Ellen Wadsworth Johnson

Hartford Election Cake and Other Receipts

Chiefly from manuscript sources

Ellen Wadsworth Johnson

Hartford Election Cake and Other Receipts
Chiefly from manuscript sources

ISBN/EAN: 9783337422899

Printed in Europe, USA, Canada, Australia, Japan

Cover: Foto ©Lupo / pixelio.de

More available books at **www.hansebooks.com**

HARTFORD
ELECTION CAKE

AND

OTHER RECEIPTS

CHIEFLY FROM MANUSCRIPT SOURCES.

COLLECTED BY

ELLEN TERRY JOHNSON.

PUBLISHED FOR THE BENEFIT OF

ST. PETER'S-IN-THE-MOUNT, HOLDERNESS, N. H.

HARTFORD, CONN.:
THE FOWLER & MILLER CO, PRINTERS, 341 MAIN STREET.
JUNE, 1889.

THE receipts included in this collection are chiefly taken from manuscript sources. Others are either framed by the collector or adapted from recipes already known.

Others still are obtained from published authorities, and either modified or found to be so valuable, by practical experience, that they are reprinted here, by the kind permission of the authors.

Every receipt in the little volume the compiler has knowledge is of value.

E. T. J.

NO. 69 VERNON STREET,
    HARTFORD, CONN.

SOUPS.

STOCK FOR SOUP.

BY PERMISSION OF CATHERINE E. OWEN

THE following rule is suitable for the preparation of stock for soup, which can be modified in many ways. It cannot fail, if carefully followed, to produce the strongest meat broth, which will be a solid jelly when cold, and which, in the estimation of many physicians, is preferable to beef tea for the use of the sick.

Put a shank of beef or veal, or both, into a soup-pot, with cold water, allowing a quart of water for each pound of meat, and salt in the proportion of a half teaspoonful to each quart of liquid. Let the soup simmer on the back of the stove for two hours; skim carefully. Put a full teaspoonful of butter into a very hot frying-pan; stir until it begins to brown, then fry in it a small onion, half a small carrot, half a turnip, and a stick or two of celery, if convenient, chopped moderately fine. When fried a light brown, add the vegetables to the soup; boil slowly three hours more. Remove from the fire, strain through fine sieve; set away until next day, when the soup should be a solid jelly from which every particle of fat can be removed.

For use, take a portion of the jelly, melt it in a small kettle, and add, if it is desired to have the soup colored, a teaspoonful of burnt sugar; if necessary, add more salt and pepper. Let it boil up once, and, having carefully skimmed the soup, serve in a hot tureen.

If rice is used to thicken the soup, boil it beforehand in a separate saucepan, and, while hot, put into the soup as it is near boiling point. If maccaroni or French paste are used, boil as directed for rice.

Always have the tureen hot before pouring in the soup. If sliced hard-boiled egg or lemon is used, or wine, place them in the tureen and pour the soup over them.

A shank of beef weighing six pounds will make soup for twelve people. If clear, serve with croûtons.

CROÛTONS.— Put a teaspoonful of butter into a very hot frying-pan; cut some dry bread into small squares or dice. When the butter is beginning to brown, add the bread, a little at a time; fry lightly; drain on a napkin, and serve in a warm dish.

Croûtons are sometimes merely dry bread, toasted slowly until quite brown, and cut into dice. Serve in a warm dish.

CALF'S HEAD SOUP.

MRS. THOS. BELKNAP.

One calf's head. The head will have been thoroughly cleaned at the butcher's, but should be carefully washed again. Remove the brains and tongue; tie the brains in a bit of muslin. Put the head, brains, and tongue in a pot; cover with four quarts of water; boil three or four hours. Strain the stock through a sieve, and set it away until the next day. Pick the meat from the bones; cover the bones with water, and boil three hours. Strain the broth, and add it to the jellied stock an hour or two before serving, with a quart can of tomatoes. Add also the bits of meat previously picked from the bones, and cut into dice, and season with one tablespoonful of whole cloves, one tablespoonful of whole allspice, one tablespoonful each of summer-savory and sweet marjoram, one tablespoonful of salt, one small onion, chopped fine. Boil gently an hour or so. Just before serving, stir into the boiling soup three tablespoonfuls of browned flour, mixed with a little stock or butter. Put into the tureen two hard-boiled eggs, sliced, and one lemon, sliced thin. Pour the soup over the egg and lemon. A wineglass of sherry or brandy may be added to the lemon and egg.

CLAM SOUP.

E. T. J.

Chop rather fine a quart of clams. Add to the liquor double the quantity of water. Let it simmer slowly on the back of the stove an hour, skimming carefully. Add the chopped clams. Let it cook slowly half an hour more. Add a pint of new milk, which, if not very carefully done, will result in curdling. Let the soup get very hot, but not boil. As you pour into the tureen, put in two teaspoonfuls of butter.

Cream, if used instead of milk, must be put in the hot tureen and the boiling soup poured over it, as, if heated, it will be apt to curdle.

CLEAR SOUP.

MRS. GEORGE HOADLEY.

Melt the stock jelly in a bright saucepan. If necessary, add more salt and pepper. Color with a teaspoonful of burnt sugar. Add the white and shell of one egg. When boiling, skim carefully; every particle of solid matter will be thus removed, and the soup be clear as sherry. Serve with croûtons.

CRANBERRY BEAN SOUP.

E. T. J.

The cranberry bean will be found preferable for soup to the turtle bean, ordinarily employed.

Soak one pint of cranberry beans over night. Boil the next morning in water until very soft. Drain off the water and rub the beans through a sieve. Add to the beans two quarts of stock. Season with a quarter teaspoonful of pepper, a half teaspoonful of salt, a tenth of a teaspoonful of powdered clove, or less. Let it boil up once. Put into the tureen two hard-boiled eggs and a small lemon, both sliced thin, and half a wineglassful of sherry. Pour the soup over them.

If you have no stock, boil a half pound of pork in two quarts of water one hour. To this the strained beans are added. If too salt, pour off the water once from the pork and add fresh. When in the tureen, stir in a large teaspoonful of butter. The pork can be cut into small dice and served with the soup, or sent whole to table on a platter.

CREAM SOUPS.

MISS CORSON.

By the old method the preparation of cream soups was a long and difficult process, but by following Miss

Corson's rule, an excellent white soup, in numberless varieties, can be prepared, when vegetables are employed.

Put any cold cooked vegetable, such as potato, young beets, tomato, peas, beans, carrots, rice, through a sieve, until you have a cupful. Put a tablespoonful butter and a tablespoonful of flour, rubbed together, into a hot saucepan. Stir over the fire until smooth and bubbling, but not brown. Stir into it, gradually, a pint of hot milk and a pint of hot water, mixed—all milk is better. Stir until quite free from lumps, then add the vegetable pulp, the salt and pepper. Let it get very hot, but not boil. Pour into hot tureen. If rice is used, a little celery, boiled and strained out, may be added.

TOMATO SOUP.

E. T. J.

Peel and cut in small pieces one quart of tomatoes. Stew in a pint of water, gently, on the back of the stove, for about an hour. When the tomato is thoroughly soft, strain through a sieve. Return to fire. When at boiling point, stir in two tablespoonfuls of butter, mixed with a tablespoonful of flour, a scant teaspoonful of salt. Add a quart of milk or a pint of cream; let it boil up a moment, then serve.

FISH.

DEVILLED CRABS.

MRS. H. W. CLOSSON.

ALTHOUGH fresh crabs are always preferable, when they can be had, those put up by the Hampton, Virginia, companies are a very good substitute. The crab shells always accompany each can of crab meat, but, as they are very brittle, there is always danger of bits of the broken shell becoming mixed with the food. The china fish or shells are safer. To the contents of one can of crab meat add three finely-powdered Boston crackers, or four tablespoonfuls of cracker meal, three tablespoonfuls of melted butter, or olive oil (the butter is better), the grated peel and juice of one lemon, two tablespoonfuls of vinegar, one hard-boiled egg, chopped fine, one well-beaten raw egg, half a teaspoonful of mustard (flour), half a teaspoonful of salt, a little pepper, red and white.

Mix thoroughly, fill the china fish or shells, scatter cracker crumbs over the top, and thickly dot it with bits of butter. Baste with a little cold water before going into the oven. Bake fifteen minutes, or until brown. This quantity will fill ten fish or shells.

DEVILLED CLAMS.

MRS. HARNICKLE.

Remove the hard part from long clams. Drain them and chop fine. Mix with the clams the same quantity of fine bread crumbs. Season with pepper; no salt will be needed, in all probability. Melt a piece of butter, in the proportion of two tablespoonfuls to a dozen clams. Wet the mixture with this and enough of the clam juice to make it quite moist, but not liquid. Wash the clam shells and rub them dry. Butter them and fill with the clam mixture, scattering fine bread crumbs over the top. Sprinkle a little water over them, and stud the surface of each with small bits of butter. Set the shells in a dripping-pan, and bake twenty minutes. Serve hot, on a napkin spread on a platter.

DEVILLED CLAMS, No. 2.

MRS. JUDGE PARKER.

Take twenty-five clams. Save the liquor. Chop the clams fine, and add four hard-boiled eggs, chopped, a quarter of the soft part of a medium-sized loaf of bread, soaked in milk; a little parsley, a large tablespoonful melted butter, salt and pepper to taste, one onion, chopped fine. Put in enough of the clam liquor to make the mixture moist, but not wet. Butter some well-washed shells, fill with the preparation of clams. Scatter bread crumbs over the top, dotted with bits of butter. Baste with a little water. Bake fifteen minutes.

CLAM CHOWDER.

MRS. JUDGE PARKER.

One dozen clams, chopped fine, three potatoes, and one onion. Boil the vegetables in a pint of water, until tender; then add the chopped clams. Let them boil up. Add the juice of the clams. Roll two soda crackers, and put in the tureen with a tablespoonful of butter. Boil one pint of milk and pour on the crackers, and then add the chowder. Season with salt and pepper.

FRICASSEED OYSTERS.

MRS. WM. EDWARDS.

Separate a quart of count oysters from the broth; place the oysters in a tightly-covered saucepan, with a quarter of a pound of good butter. Set on the back of the stove, where it will simmer gently until the oysters are done. Cook the broth in another saucepan, with three tablespoonfuls of powdered cracker, and a little pepper. When the oysters are done, remove them with a fork from the butter, place them on toasted crackers, on a platter. Add the butter to the oyster broth, let it boil up once, add a half pint of cream, and pour over the oysters.

OYSTER PATÉS.

The paté shells are best procured from a confectioner.

Use small oysters, pour off half the liquor, cook slowly, on the back of the stove, adding to the oysters powdered cracker in the proportion of three spoonfuls to a pint of liquid. Add a little white pepper. When the oysters are done, skim them out into a hot bowl. Cook the oyster broth ten minutes longer, until quite smooth and thick. Add a little cream, not enough to thin the broth, a very little nutmeg, and, as you take it from the fire, a good-sized bit of butter. Pour over the oysters. Heat the paté shells; fill with the oysters and cream sauce, which can be also poured over the paté before sending to table, or only enough used to fill the cavity. The little cover should close the opening when the shell is filled. Serve on hot platter.

TURBOT À LA CRÊME.

ADAPTED BY E. T. J

Make a pint or more of white sauce. Pick to fine bits two pounds of cold boiled fresh cod, or other white fish. Fill a well-buttered pudding dish (the blue Japanese bowls are excellent for this purpose), mixing with the cod a half pint of oysters, chopped fine, and alternating the layer of fish with one of white sauce. Sprinkle a little salt over the layers of cod. Scatter bread or cracker crumbs over the top of the dish, when full, and little bits of butter. Baste, before going into the oven, with a little cold water. Cook twenty minutes, or until the top is browned.

TURBOT OR FISH AU GRATIN.

ADAPTED BY E. T. J.

Pick in flakes a pound and a half of cold boiled cod or halibut, or any firm white fish. Place a layer of it in a buttered dish; cover it with a layer of white sauce, made by stirring two tablespoonfuls butter in a saucepan over the fire, adding a tablespoonful of flour; when it bubbles, being stirred constantly, pour in a pint of milk or water, hot. Flavor with a little salt and a little lemon juice, a teaspoonful, if desired. When quite thick, remove from fire. Have two or three hard-boiled eggs, chopped fine; scatter a little over the layer of sauce. Put more fish, sauce, and egg, alternately, until the dish is full. Scatter bread or cracker crumbs on top. Dot the crumbs with small bits of butter, and baste with a little milk or water, just as it goes into the oven. Bake until the top is brown, not over ten or fifteen minutes.

MEATS.

THE secret of properly roasting meat is to have a quick, hot fire on placing it in the oven, that the surface being at once scorched, may retain the juices. After half an hour's quick roasting, the heat should be gradually diminished, until the ordinary temperature for roasting meat is attained. All roast meats should be constantly basted with the contents of the dripping-pan, and poultry may be dredged with flour when put in the oven. Very thin slices of salt pork, not bacon, which imparts a smoky flavor, may be tied over the breast of game birds, and removed before serving.

BRAISED BEEF.
MRS. H. W. CLOSSON.

Take a piece, four inches thick, of the round of beef, from the upper part; put it into a pot, with enough water to half cover it. Let it simmer gently three hours; when thoroughly tender, remove the beef to a hot platter. Season the gravy in the pot with salt and pepper. Strain into it a pint of stewed tomato. Stir well, and let it boil up once. Add a tablespoonful of butter, and pour over the meat in the dish. If used a second day, take the meat only, warm it in a pint of stock; thicken this with stewed tomato and serve as before.

CHICKEN CROQUETTES.

MRS. A. R. TERRY.

Cut off the meat of two boiled or roast chickens, remove skin and fat, and chop fine. Put a quarter of a pound of butter into a porcelain kettle; when it bubbles up, stir in two tablespoonfuls flour, one teaspoonful salt, one teaspoonful of black pepper, two-thirds of a nutmeg, one teacup of chicken broth, the broth in which the chickens were cooked, boiled down to half its quantity, or a little soup made of the bones of the roast chickens off which the meat has been chopped; mix well together; mould it with the hands into croquettes; dip each into beaten egg, then into fine cracker crumbs. Set them in a cool place, to harden, before frying light brown, in boiling lard.

In frying croquettes, doughnuts, or Saratoga potatoes, the first object to be attained is to have a large quantity of lard very hot, and kept at that point. The heat can be ascertained by dropping a bit of bread in,

CHICKEN CROQUETTES, No. 2.

MRS. GEORGE HOADLEY.

Boil a chicken tender, remove skin and bones, and chop fine. Wet with some white meat soup or with drawn butter. Season with salt, pepper, mace, lemon peel and juice. Have the mixture as soft as it can be moulded. Dip in beaten egg, then in cracker crumbs, and fry in boiling lard.

CHICKEN SHORTCAKE.

MRS. ROSE TERRY COOKE.

Joint and stew two fowls till tender, peppering them well. When done, carefully take the flesh from the bones, separating it from every bit of fat, skin, sinew or gristle. Return this to the gravy, and set aside till cold; then skim off all the fat, pour off the gravy, put it in a saucepan, flavor it with salt, celery salt, and a little nutmeg. Melt a large spoonful of butter in a pan, stir into it two large spoonfuls of flour, till smooth; set the gravy aside, where it will not boil, and mix a little of it, slowly, with the flour and butter. Too much haste or heat will make lumps. When all is added to the gravy, return to the saucepan, and boil till it thickens well, stirring constantly. If onion is not disliked add a small one to the fowls, during the first boiling, but skim it out of the gravy on leaving that to cool. Make a cake of one quart flour, one teaspoonful salt, three teaspoons Royal baking powder, butter size of an egg. Sift salt, flour, and powder together; then rub in the butter and add milk, to make a soft dough. Roll out a thin square or oblong sheet, the size of your platter, and bake till well done. Cut the rest of the dough into very small rounds, and bake at the same time. When done, split the large cake, butter it, dip out the chicken with a strainer, heap it evenly on one-half the cake, cover with the other, and pour the gravy over all. Put the small biscuit about the edge of the platter, for garnish.

CHICKEN SHORTCAKE, No. 2.

MISS CHARLOTTE M. ELY.

Mix two teaspoonfuls Royal baking powder with one pint of flour. Rub into it a small half cup of butter, and wet it with a cup of sweet milk.

Bake in a quick oven, in a thin sheet.

Proceed as in receipt given above.

This shortcake receipt is excellent for use with strawberries. It is quite as good with only one and a half teaspoonfuls of baking powder to the pint of flour.

CHICKEN JELLY.

BRIDGET PLUNKETT.

Joint the chicken, cover it with water, and let it simmer, gently, until the meat will come from the bones easily. Strain, and set the liquid to cool. When cold, skim off the fat carefully; add half a box of gelatine, warming the chicken liquid slightly, to allow of its mixing. Pick the meat from the bones, cutting it in small pieces. Season with a little cayenne, salt, and the juice of a lemon. Add two hard-boiled eggs and a lemon, cut in thin slices. Arrange in the mould in any fanciful pattern. Fill the mould with the prepared chicken, and pour the liquid over it.

CHICKEN CURRY.

A RESIDENT OF INDIA, THROUGH MISS KING.

Two large teaspoonfuls turmeric powder; one-third of a teaspoonful of shelled cardamon seeds; one small teaspoonful cayenne pepper; one teaspoonful fine salt; a few bits of cinnamon; a small piece of green ginger, sliced; four small cloves of garlic; one grated cocoanut; one pint of milk.

All the spices to be pounded separately, then well mixed, the grated cocoanut to be added.

Pour over these a pint of warm water, and let it simmer until the water is pretty well absorbed. Then add the milk, warm.

Rub together a large tablespoonful of butter and a little flour, and brown it; add to the other ingredients. The chicken must be well boiled, and then jointed and cut in pieces. Put it in the curry mixture; let it boil up once, to thoroughly heat it. Stir the curry well before adding chicken.

LUNCH DISH.

MRS. HEMAN ELY.

Take a pound of veal steak, removing skin and fat. Cover with a quart of water and let it slowly simmer until the liquid is reduced to one pint. Take out the meat, when very tender, cut it into dice. Prepare a mould, by first wetting it in cold water. Boil hard and slice thin two eggs, place them with the veal, and a few thin slices of lemon, in the mould, when the liquid is ready. Season with a half teaspoonful of salt, a tiny pinch of nutmeg, an eighth of a teaspoonful of pepper, a very little powdered clove. Strain the broth into the mould. Set on ice and turn out on a platter. Should the liquid refuse to jelly, reheat it and add to the above quantity an eighth of a box of Nelson's gelatine.

LUNCH DISH.

MRS. PECHIN.

Boil tender two chickens; cut into dice the white meat and a little of the dark. Simmer gently, on the back of the stove, a quart of cream, with one very small onion, a little mace, salt, and pepper. Thicken it with a tablespoonful of butter, stirred into a roux, with two teaspoonfuls of flour. The consistence of the liquid should be that of thick cream. Meanwhile, stew a can of French mushrooms, gently, for an hour, in a pint of stock, or until the liquid is reduced to less than half its original quantity. Boil, until tender, a pair of sweet breads or more, cut them in dice; butter a large dish; place on the bottom a layer of the chicken, then of mushrooms, cut in half, then of sweet breads. Pour over it some of the thickened cream, and fill the dish with the alternate layers, in the order named. Scatter bread crumbs over the top, with little bits of butter. Bake an hour.

TIMBALE.

MISS PARLOA.

Chop fine any kind of cold dark meat — cold stewed beef, roast beef, veal, mutton, game. Mix with it a quarter teaspoonful of pepper, half a pickled onion, chopped fine, a teaspoonful of chopped parsley, a cup of stock or milk, two tablespoonfuls of butter, melted while stirred constantly, to prevent oiling, half a cupful of fine bread crumbs, a half teaspoonful of salt. Mix the seasoning with the meat and bread crumbs. Add the stock and two well-beaten eggs. The eggs must be thoroughly incorporated with the mixture or it will present an unsightly appearance when cooked. Put into a well-buttered pan—an oval charlotte russe pan is the best. Set it into a pan of boiling water; cover with a bit of buttered paper. Cook ten or fifteen minutes. Turn out on a hot platter. A brown sauce may be poured over it, or it will be found very good without it.

TO ROAST QUAILS.

After thoroughly cleansing the birds, and, if desired, stuffing them with bread crumbs, salt and pepper, moistened with melted butter, tie thin slices of fat salt pork over the breast. Place them in a baking pan and set in a quick oven, basting them at first with a little melted butter, then with the drippings in the pan. Roast twenty or twenty-five minutes. Fifteen minutes before they are done, place a small square of buttered toast under each bird, to receive the gravy dropping from it. Send the quail to the table, each on its bit of toast, on a hot platter.

RISSOLES.

ADAPTED FROM MRS. HENDERSON.

Roll a sheet of puff paste out a quarter inch thick; make a preparation of minced chicken, veal, or the tenderloin of beef, cut very fine. Heat two or three tablespoonfuls of cream with the same quantity of stock; when very hot, stir into it a large teaspoonful of butter and the same quantity of flour, rubbed together. When quite smooth, add a quarter of a teaspoonful of pepper, a half teaspoonful of salt, a very little nutmeg. When the gravy is quite hot, add the meat. Let it get thoroughly hot, but not cook.

Place teaspoonfuls of the mixture about three inches from the edge of the paste, three inches apart. Fold the paste over and strike the edge of the hand between each one. Cut out the rissoles with a small tumbler. Bake, in a very quick oven, five minutes.

BEEF HASH.

DAVID S. S. C. JONES.

The prejudice against re-cooked meat is well founded. Meat served a second time should never be more than warmed over, and with this fact thoroughly understood, it will be found perfectly digestible.

In preparing minced meat, stock should, if possible, be employed. But whether stock or water forms the foundation of the gravy, it should be allowed to become boiling hot in the saucepan. Thicken it when boiling, with a roux of a tablespoonful of butter, rubbed together with a full teaspoonful of flour, to a half pint of gravy. Let it bubble, stirring until quite smooth. Season with salt, pepper, and whatever spice may be appropriate to the meat used. Turn in the mince, stirring it well but lightly in. Let it become very hot, but not boil for a moment. Turn the hash out upon a hot dish, on buttered toast.

Excellent hash can be made from cold steak, braised or roasted beef. Mince it finely, rejecting the skin and fat. Prepare the gravy of stock, as already described. Cold gravy should never be used in warming over meat. Warm the beef in the stock. Season with salt and pepper only. Serve on a hot dish, with a circle of hot boiled rice about it.

VEAL MINCE.

Chop the veal very fine. Make a gravy of a cup of stock. Season with salt, pepper, and a very little powdered mace or nutmeg. When very hot, thicken with a tablespoonful of butter, stirred with a scant teaspoonful of flour. When smooth, add the minced veal, and when hot, stir in a little cream, as you take it from the fire. Serve on slices of buttered toast, on a hot platter. Put thin slices of lemon on top.

MUTTON HASH.
DAVID S. S. C. JONES.

Prepare the gravy as for beef hash. Cut the cold roast or boiled mutton in small pieces, with an equal quantity of cold boiled potato, removing skin and fat. The quantity of gravy should be greater for this than for mince. Only heat the meat and potato thoroughly, and serve in a hot dish.

' TURKEY HASH.
PLATTSBURGH COOK BOOK.

Two pounds cold roast or boiled turkey—white meat only. Chop it rather fine, and chop with it one head of celery, boiled tender.

Boil a quart of cream; when boiling, add a little salt and pepper, thicken with a roux, then put in the turkey and celery. Let the mince become thoroughly hot, not boil; then pour upon slices of buttered toast, upon a hot platter.

Toast, for such purposes, should be well browned. Melt two tablespoonfuls of butter, by pouring upon it four tablespoonfuls of boiling water, and dip the slices of toast into it, that they may become somewhat soft. Use more butter and water, if you have a large number of slices.

VEGETABLES.

STEWED MACARONI.

MRS. H. W. CLOSSON.

BOIL tender half a pound of medium-sized macaroni; when soft, add half a pound of cheese, broken in small pieces, and a little butter. Put in a hot dish, and, when serving, pour over the whole a pint of tomato sauce.

STEWED MACARONI, No. 2.

OLIVE HARPER.

Cook one-third of a pound of macaroni in a pint of clear beef soup. Let it cook, gently, fifteen minutes; add a saltspoonful salt. Take up the macaroni, put it on the dish in which it is to be served. Sprinkle grated cheese thickly over it. Pour over the whole a pint of tomato sauce, and send at once to table.

SARATOGA POTATOES.

MRS. VAN REED.

Slice the potatoes very thin; let them stand in ice-water for a few hours, changing the water three or four times. Spread the slices on a soft coarse towel. Have a frying-pan two-thirds full of lard—a small, deep iron kettle is still better. Heat the lard very hot, testing it by dropping in it a bit of the potato; if the fat is hot enough, the slice will immediately puff up and rise to the surface. Pull the slices of potato carefully apart, and fry two dozen or so at a time. Turn them with a fork. They will be done in one minute, if the fat is sufficiently hot. Take them from the kettle with a skimmer; drain in a colander, or on sheets of blotting paper. Dust a little salt over them, while hot.

SCOLLOPED POTATOES.

MRS. GEO. WILLEY.

Slice the raw potatoes thin into a well-buttered dish. Pour in enough milk to half fill the dish. Season with salt, and add a heaping tablespoonful of butter cut into little bits. Bake very slowly, covering the dish with a plate until twenty minutes before serving. Let it then color a pale brown.

STUFFED POTATOES.

DAVID S. S. C. JONES.

Select large, smooth potatoes, as nearly as possible of a uniform size. Bake until thoroughly done, but be careful not to over cook them. Cut the top carefully off; with a small silver fork, scrape the contents of each potato into a warm bowl, taking care not to break the skin. Mash the potato with the fork, adding salt to taste, and a good teaspoonful of butter to each potato. When thoroughly mixed, return the potato to the skins, heaping it high, but not smoothing it. Set the potatoes up on end, in the dish in which you serve them; return them to the oven to warm, but avoid browning them.

If you prefer it, the covers can be replaced on the potatoes and retained by a narrow ribbon.

These potatoes are excellent with broiled shad or pompanos.

STEWED TOMATOES.

MRS. VAN REED.

The southern method of stewing tomatoes is a great improvement upon the ordinary way.

Put a large tablespoonful of butter into a very hot frying-pan; when boiling, fry in the butter one-half an onion, or one small onion, chopped fine, to a light brown. Then pour into the pan a can of tomatoes, or a quart of the fresh vegetable, cut in small pieces. Let it stew gently an hour, seasoning it with salt and pepper. Thicken with half a cup of fine bread crumbs.

BAKED TOMATOES.

MRS. C. A. TERRY.

Butter a baking dish; cover the bottom with a layer of tomatoes, cut in small pieces. On this place a layer of fine bread crumbs. Season this with pepper, salt, a very little nutmeg, and small bits of butter scattered over the bread. Repeat until the dish is full, having the top layer of bread crumbs, and thickly scattered with bits of butter. The top may be basted with a little cold water, before going into the oven. It will take a quarter of a pound of butter to properly prepare this dish. Bake an hour or more, covering the top with card-board for the first half hour.

STUFFED TOMATOES.

MRS. H. W. CLOSSON.

Take fine, large tomatoes, of equal size; cut out the stem end, and, with a sharp knife, remove a portion of the inside, leaving a quarter inch of thickness. Stuff with any kind of meat, chopped very fine, seasoned with salt and pepper, and mixed with a quarter its quantity of fine bread crumbs, made soft with melted butter. Set the tomatoes in a baking pan, put a little hot water in the bottom, to prevent burning; baste, while baking, with a little melted butter and hot water, mixed. Serve in hot dish.

BREAD, BISCUITS, ETC.

BISCUIT.

MRS. HOWARD.

THE YEAST.—Three quarts lukewarm water; a handful of hops; three potatoes, boiled five minutes and grated; one-third cup of salt; one-third cup of sugar, white; flour enough to make a thin batter. Boil the hops in the water, add the grated potato and flour; when cool, add one-half cup of yeast; when white on the top, stir.

THE BISCUIT.—Two cups of milk; one tablespoonful of butter; one-half teaspoonful salt; one tablespoonful sugar, white; one-half cup of yeast. Make up the sponge early in the morning, and let it rise. When light, cut down and mould. Let it rise again, then mould into small rolls, place them in a pan, and let them rise an hour and a half, before baking.

SOUTHERN CORN BREAD.

MRS. THOS. WAYNE.

One pint corn meal; three eggs, beaten separately; a small bit of butter; two teaspoonfuls of baking powder; one cup cold boiled rice or hominy; milk to make a thin batter. Bake in a loaf or in gem pans.

SOUTHERN BISCUITS.

MRS. THOS. WAYNE.

One tablespoonful lard; one tablespoonful butter; cut up with a knife or rubbed fine with the tips of cool fingers. [*1 qt of sifted flour*] Wet with milk or water, to make a dough like pie crust, mixing with a knife. Roll out very thin, cut with the top of a claret glass or small cutter. Prick and bake ten minutes, in a very hot oven.

These are the true Southern short biscuits, without beating; crisp, light, and which will keep for weeks. They are excellent to take to sea, or upon a journey.

In the hands of a Southern cook, they require no baking powder; but it is safer to use a teaspoonful and a half of baking powder.

The success depends upon the thinness of the biscuit and the heat of the fire.

BEST CREAM PUFFS.

MRS. B. F. D. ADAMS.

One pint of cream; one pint flour; three eggs, beaten separately; a half teaspoonful of salt. Bake in gem pans, in a very hot oven.

EGG PUFFS.

MRS. JUDGE PARKER.

One pint milk; three eggs; six tablespoonfuls flour. Beat well together. Bake in hot cups.

BROWN BREAD.

LYDIA TALBOT.

Two cups unsifted rye flour; two cups sifted Indian meal; one cup sifted white flour; three-quarters cup molasses; one teaspoonful salt; one pint of milk and water; one teaspoonful soda. Steam four hours in mould.

BROWN BREAD, No. 2.

MRS. JUDGE PARKER.

One pint warm milk; half a cup of molasses; one teaspoonful soda, dissolved in a very little warm water; half a teaspoonful salt. Stir in enough graham flour to make a stiff batter, as for bread. Add half a cake of compressed yeast. Beat long and hard. Let it rise over night. When light, stir in enough graham flour to make it like common bread. Put in pans to rise. Bake half an hour.

This is a better rule for brown bread than is found in any receipt book.

BOSTON BROWN BREAD.
MRS. JUDGE PARKER.

Two cups corn meal; one cup rye flour; two cups sweet milk; one cup sour milk; two-thirds cup molasses; one teaspoonful soda, put into the molasses; a little salt. Put in a round tin and steam three hours. Do not cover the pan.

GRAHAM GEMS.
MISS WOOLSEY.

One pint of milk or water; one pint of sifted graham flour; a half teaspoonful salt. Beat well. Heat the gem pans very hot. Bake in a very hot oven.

BROWN SCONES.
WASHINGTON COOKING SCHOOL.

One pound wheaten flour; six ounces butter; a little salt. Wet with thick cream. Roll out and cut in thin cakes. Bake on a griddle.

WHEAT MUFFINS.
MRS. CHAS. A. TERRY.

One quart sour milk; one tablespoonful melted butter; one tablespoonful sugar; one teaspoonful soda; two eggs, beaten separately; flour to make a thin batter; one cup cold boiled rice or hominy, broken up fine with a fork. Bake in hot muffin pans.

These muffins can be made of sweet milk, using two small teaspoonfuls of baking powder, instead of soda.

If two-thirds sour and one-third sweet milk is used, take three-fourths teaspoonful of soda, three-fourths spoonful of baking powder.

WAFFLES.

MRS. H. W. CLOSSON.

One quart sweet milk; one teacup cold boiled rice or fine hominy; two eggs, well beaten; one teaspoonful sugar; two teaspoonfuls lard or butter, melted; half teaspoonful salt; one small teaspoonful soda: two small teaspoonfuls cream of tartar, or instead of these use two teaspoonfuls of baking powder; flour to make a thin batter, about a pint or more.

CAKE.

BOSWELL CAKE.

MR. BOSWELL, EAST HARTFORD.

TEN cups of flour; six cups of sugar; three cups of butter; eight eggs; three cups warm milk and one wineglass of rum in it; one teaspoonful of soda, dissolved in a little of the milk; two pounds of raisins; nutmeg, or mace. Bake an hour and a half.

DELICATE CAKE.

MRS. C. A. TERRY.

Half pound butter; three-fourths pound flour; one pound sugar; whites of fourteen eggs. Rub together the butter and flour. Add the sugar, which has been stirred lightly into the well-beaten whites of the eggs. Stir well. Flavor with bitter almond. Bake in oblong sponge-cake pans, with buttered paper.

IMPERIAL CAKE.

MRS. G. V. WEIR.

One pound butter; one pound sugar; one pound flour; one pound raisins; three-fourths pound almonds, blanced and slit; three-fourths pound citron; one pound currants, if desired; one wineglass of brandy and rose water (not extract of rose); the juice and rind of a lemon. Rub the butter and sugar to a cream, with a little rose water. One small teaspoonful mace improves the flavor. Beat the eggs separately.

This makes three loaves.

Bake, in a bread oven, about an hour.

A third of a teaspoonful of soda, or less, improves it, as there is so much fruit in it.

HARTFORD ELECTION CAKE YEAST.

MRS. SHELDON.

Three pints of water; eight good-sized potatoes, peeled and cut in slices.

Boil in the water with a small handful of hops, until tender. Rub through a sieve. Pour the boiling water in which the potatoes were cooked upon the strained potatoes, through a sieve.

Stir in enough flour to make a stiff batter.

Make the batter very sweet with brown sugar.

Add a coffee cup of distiller's yeast.

Let it rise twenty-four hours before using.

Where the use of domestic yeast is impracticable, that obtained from the distillery can be substituted.

It has been claimed that the compressed yeast of modern use, is worthless for making election cake. This is incorrect, for although it is undoubtedly less successful, as a rule, still excellent loaf cake has been made of it. It requires a cake and a half of Fleischman's yeast to raise seven loaves of cake.

ELECTION CAKE, No. 1.

MRS. SHELDON.

Eight pounds flour; four and a quarter pounds butter; four and a quarter pounds sugar; five eggs; one quart home-made yeast; four pounds raisins; one pound citron; one ounce mace; one ounce nutmeg; new milk to make the batter sufficiently thin; one tumbler mixed wine and brandy.

Beat to a cream the butter and sugar.

Mix half of it with the flour at two o'clock in the afternoon, wet with the new milk, slightly warm. The batter should be thinner than biscuit dough. Add the yeast; a little salt. Let it rise. When light, at night, add all other ingredients, with balance of butter and sugar. Let it rise again; then put in pans, making ten medium-sized loaves. Let it rise an hour.

ELECTION CAKE, No. 2.

MISS REBECCA BUTLER.

Eight quarts flour; three and a half pounds sugar; three pounds butter; five eggs; one quart home-made yeast; three quarts milk; six pounds raisins; half ounce mace; half ounce nutmeg; half pint wine.

ELECTION CAKE, No. 3.

MRS. LEWIS WELD.

Four and a half pounds of flour; two and a half pounds of sugar; two and a quarter pounds of butter; four eggs; half ounce nutmeg; half ounce mace; one tumblerful brandy and wine; two pounds raisins; half pound citron.

At noon, or early in the afternoon, begin making this cake. Rub together the butter and flour; wet it with one quart of milk, lukewarm, and either a half pint distillers' yeast or one cake and a half of compressed yeast. Beat well, cover the pan with a cloth and set in a warm place to rise. At night, when very light, add the sugar, spice, and eggs. Set the pan in a moderately warm place. Early next morning, add the fruit and wine, the grated peel of a lemon, half a teaspoonful extract of rose. Put into pans covered with buttered paper. Let them stand an hour, then put in as many as the oven will hold, selecting the smallest pans to bake first. A half teaspoonful of soda, dissolved in a little warm water, will be safe. This receipt makes seven loaves, which require to bake an hour or more.

ELECTION CAKE, No. 4.

MRS. NATHANIEL TERRY.

Twelve quarts of flour; six pounds of sugar; six pounds of butter; twelve eggs; one pint wine and brandy; one quart hop yeast; six pounds raisins; one ounce mace; three ounces nutmeg.

This cake is put together as directed in the preceding receipt, except that half only of the butter is mixed with the flour, in making the sponge. The remaining butter is added with the sugar, when worked over at night.

The receipt makes twelve loaves.

ELECTION CAKE, No. 5.

MRS. HENRY HUDSON.

Four and a half pounds sugar; four and a quarter pounds butter; one peck sifted flour; two quarts of milk; six eggs; four and a half pounds raisins; half pint wine; half pint brandy; nutmeg, and mace.

The yeast for this cake is preferably home made, for

which the receipt has already been given. The quantity is three-fourths of a quart, and the cake is mixed as in Receipt No. 3.

ELECTION CAKE, No. 6.

MISS C. M. ELY.

Two quarts flour; one and a half pounds sugar; one pound butter and lard; one pint home-made yeast; one pint or more new milk. one egg; one wineglass (sherry) of brandy and wine, mixed; two nutmegs; one pound raisins.

Mix at 2 P.M., adding half the butter and sugar, worked to a cream, with yeast, milk, a little salt, and all the flour. When light, at evening, work in the rest of the materials. Beat well. Let it rise over night, and, in the morning, work over, put in pans, and let it rise an hour. Bake in moderate oven. Frost the loaves.

ELECTION CAKE, No. 7.

WINDSOR, CONN.

Six pounds flour; three and a half pounds sugar; two and a half pounds butter and lard, beaten to a cream.

Take the flour and half the shortening, with one and a half cups of good yeast and milk enough to make a stiff batter. Let it rise over night, then add the rest of the shortening, and let it rise again. When light, add nutmeg, mace, half a pint of St. Croix rum, one and a half pounds of raisins, one orange, a pound of citron. Add the well-beaten whites of two eggs, two teaspoonfuls of baking powder. Put the batter in the pans; allow it to rise an hour.

ELECTION CAKE, No. 8.

MRS. CHARLES H. BRAINARD.

It is essensial for this cake that the yeast should be made expressly for it.

Boil one potato in a pint of water; ten minutes before it is soft, add a teaspoonful of hops. The water should be reduced one-half. Rub the potato through a hair sieve, and, when cool, add to the hop water one-sixth of a Fleischman yeast cake and four tablespoonfuls of flour, taken from that weighed out for the cake. Rub smooth, stir into the liquid, and let the whole rise, adding a half teaspoonful of salt.

THE CAKE — The receipt, in full, makes fourteen loaves, and is usually divided.

Eight pounds pastry flour; four and a half pounds sugar; four and a half pounds butter (part Deerfoot or Strawberry Hill lard can be used); six pounds raisins;

two pounds citron; two pounds currants or Sultana raisins; one ounce nutmeg; half ounce mace; eight eggs; one and a half gills of brandy; one and a half gills of wine; three pints milk; the juice of one or two oranges and a little grated peel.

At noon, rub well together the butter and sugar, until like pudding sauce.

Mix well half of this with the flour; add the milk, which must be lukewarm; a teaspoonful of salt; the eggs, and lastly, the yeast. Beat it half an hour. Set in warm place. By ten o'clock it will be light. Add the remaining butter and sugar, wine, brandy, spices, and orange juice. Beat half an hour. Set it in a warm place until morning. Stir into it, very lightly, the fruit, well dredged with flour, which must be taken from that measured for the cake.

Let it stand in the pans, which must be lined with buttered paper, an hour and a half before baking. It must not be stirred in the oven, nor the place of the pans changed.

Frost the loaves. The pans must be filled two-thirds full. The batter must be very thin; if too stiff, warm with a little warm milk.

ELECTION CAKE, No. 9.

"CHOICE RECEIPTS."

Four pounds flour; two pounds sugar; one pound lard; one pound butter; two pounds raisins; one pound citron; four eggs; one quart of new milk; two heaping teaspoonfuls mace; four nutmegs; a tumblerful of wine and brandy; one pint home-made yeast.

In the morning, cream the butter and lard, and, when very light, add the sugar, mixing well. Take a little less than half the butter and rub well into the flour, which should be well warmed; add the milk, slightly warmed, and the yeast. Mix thoroughly, and let it stand where it will keep warm until it becomes very light, which should be about nine or ten o'clock at night. Do not disturb it while rising.

Beat the eggs separately and mix with the remainder of the shortening, adding the spice and wine, etc. Mix well, and let it rise a second time. In the morning, when light, fill the pans two-thirds full, putting in a little at a time, and dropping the fruit in thickly in layers. Bake in a slow oven.

THE YEAST —Boil a small handful of hops in one quart of water, strain through a sieve; pour, boiling hot, over the flour, to make a thin batter. When cool, add a half pint of distillery yeast; strain again, and let it stand until very light and foaming. Make the yeast the day before it is to be used.

ELECTION CAKE, No. 10, PLAIN.

MISS MARY ANN OLCOTT.

Three cups of new milk, warm; one cup sugar; one cup home-made yeast.

At two o'clock P.M. make a stiff batter, and let it rise. Beat well, and add, about bed time, three cups of sugar; two cups of butter; half cup sweet lard; one egg; one pound raisins; half pound citron, sliced thin; three nutmegs; four teaspoonfuls mace, powdered; half wineglass brandy; half wineglass wine.

ELECTION CAKE, No. 11.

MISS GLEASON.

Ten cups of flour; four cups milk; two cups sugar; one cup home-made yeast, or two-thirds of a cup of distillers' yeast, omitting a little to add in the morning.

Beat the batter well. Let it rise over night.

Take two cups of sugar; three cups butter; two eggs.

Add the balance of yeast and these ingredients to the batter; beat very hard, and, when well mixed, let it rise again. When very light, add half ounce of nutmeg and a quarter ounce of mace; two pounds raisins; one pound citron; one teaspoonful of soda; two teaspoonfuls of cream tartar; one wineglass of brandy.

Let the cake rise again, in the pans, before putting it in the oven.

QUICK LOAF CAKE.

MISS H. W. TERRY.

One and a half pounds flour; half pound butter; three-fourths pound sugar; three eggs; one glass of wine; one cup of milk; half a nutmeg; half a teaspoonful cinnamon; two teaspoonfuls baking powder; one pound raisins.

MADELINES.

ADAPTED BY E. T. J.

These delicious little cakes can be either made of very rich batter, in which case they can be kept much longer, or after a simpler receipt.

Three-quarters pound of butter; one pound sugar; one pound flour; nine eggs; half wineglass brandy; grated peel of one lemon; half grated nutmeg; half teaspoonful Royal baking powder.

Stir butter to a cream, add sugar, beat well. Add the beaten yolks of eggs alternately, with half the flour, then the beaten whites with the balance of flour. The brandy, spices, and lemon may be added to sugar and butter, when beaten well. Sift the baking powder in the flour before adding eggs. Butter two or three dripping pans well. Pour in the batter half an inch thick. Fill as many pans as the oven will hold. The mixture will bake in ten minutes in a moderate oven.

When it has been out of the oven two minutes, cut it in squares with a warm knife. Spread each square with either strawberry, raspberry, apricot, or green gage jam (the very acid kinds will not do), or chopped crystalized fruits, or chopped blanched nuts. On this drop from a spoon a thick layer of soft frosting, taking care that it does not run down the sides. Make the frosting as follows:

To the white of one egg, take a heaping cup of powdered sugar, stir it in without first beating the egg, add three drops of rose water, five of vanilla, and the juice of a quarter of a lemon.

MADELINES, No. 2.

ADAPTED BY E. T. J.

One cup butter; two cups sugar; two-thirds cup milk; six eggs; two small teaspoonfuls baking powder; two and a half cups flour. Flavor with half a glass brandy, half a nutmeg, and the grated rind of a lemon.

Bake as directed in preceding receipt, and use the jam and frosting in the same way. These are very delicate and light, but will not keep as long as madelines made of richer cake.

"FIVE O'CLOCKS."

E. T. J.

One cup of butter; two cups of sugar; three cups of sifted flour; four eggs, beaten separately; half cup milk or sour cream — if cream is used, add a quarter teaspoonful of soda; half a nutmeg; ten drops rose water; grated peel of one lemon; one dessertspoonful vanilla; one glass sherry or half glass brandy; half a pound of citron, cut fine.

Stir butter and sugar together, add the wine, flavoring, and lemon peel. Stir in the milk, alternately, with half the flour. Add two level teaspoofuls baking powder in a little of the flour. Stir in the beaten eggs, alternately, with the remaining flour, reserving a very little to dredge the citron.

Lastly, add the fruit. Half a pound of raisins may be used, if desired. Bake in small block-tin pattypans. This receipt makes sixty cakes. Frost with the Asquam frosting. Two eggs will frost all.

ASQUAM FROSTING.

E. T. J.

To the white of one egg, take one and a quarter cups of pulverized sugar. Stir in the sugar without beating the egg. Add three drops rose water, ten of vanilla, and the juice of half a lemon. It will at once become very white, and will harden in a very few moments, which is its chief claim to distinction.

BLACK CAKE.

MRS. G. V. N. LOTHROP.

Two pounds butter; two pounds sugar; two pounds flour; five pounds raisins; five pounds currants; two pounds citron; twenty eggs; one tumblerful brandy; one tumblerful wine; one tablespoonful cloves; two tablespoonfuls cinnamon; two tablespoonfuls mace.

BLACK CAKE, No. 2.

MRS. DAVENPORT.

Thirteen pounds raisins; three pounds preserved lemon peel; three pounds citron; five pounds currants; four pounds butter; six pounds sugar; four pounds flour; thirty-six eggs; two ounces mace, ground; half ounce nutmeg; half box cinnamon, ground; half box cloves; one pint molasses; two and a half pints whiskey and wine.

This is absolutely perfect cake, and has been tried many times. The receipt given makes about fifty pounds. One-quarter of the receipt is enough for ordinary occasions. Do not attempt to bake it in the house, but send to a baker.

ANGEL CAKE.

HOTEL CAPITOL, HARTFORD.

Whites of eight eggs, well beaten; one cup pulverized sugar; half cup flour; half cup corn starch; one teaspoonful baking powder, sifted with flour, sugar, and starch; add eggs. Flavor with lemon.

FRUIT CAKE.

MRS. WM. THOMPSON.

One pound flour; one pound sugar; one pound butter; one pound eggs; two pounds raisins; two pounds currants; half pound citron; mace, nutmeg, cinnamon, and cloves, one-half ounce each; one glass of brandy; half teaspoonful soda.

SPONGE CAKE.

MRS. FORD.

Twelve eggs; the weight of ten eggs in powdered sugar, and the weight of five large eggs in flour; the grated peel of a large lemon and half the juice.

Stir together the yolks of eggs, and sugar till very light. A wooden spoon or a Dover egg beater will do best to beat with. When light, add the lemon peel and juice.

Beat the whites very light, and stir in gently, but thoroughly, with a silver fork.

Sift the flour in, in three instalments, stirring it in as lightly as consistent with thorough mixing. Practice will give the best peculiar movement of the fork or spoon which scatters the flour, while mixing it in. If the eggs are large, this quantity will make a large milk pan loaf and two oblong bread pan loaves. If the eggs are small, the quantity will fill the milk pan, and is much the best way to bake it. Line the pan with stiff white paper, making the sides straight. Bake an hour, in a moderate oven, watching carefully, to avoid burning.

This cake is the handsomest of all sponge cakes.

SPONGE CAKE, No. 2.

MISS WOOLSEY.

Twelve eggs; the weight of twelve in sugar, and of six in flour; the grated peel and juice of one lemon. Proceed as in the first receipt. The preponderance of sugar makes the cake less handsome than the first receipt, but moister, and with a sugary crust on top.

If sponge cake is frosted, the icing should be flavored with lemon juice.

SPONGE CAKE, No. 3.

MRS. ROSE TERRY COOKE.

Nine eggs, ten if small; one pound pulverized sugar; half pound flour (pastry); the juice and peel, grated, of a lemon. Add the sugar to the whites, sifting it in, and beating it in with a fork.

Add the yolks next, then the flour, lastly, the lemon juice and peel.

Line the pans with buttered paper. Bake in a moderate oven. When the cake is in the oven, sit down by the oven door, and watch till it is done.

COCOANUT CAKE.

MISS FARRAN.

One cup of butter; two cups of sugar; two-thirds cup of milk; whites of six eggs; yolks of four eggs; two and a half cups of flour; two teaspoonfuls baking powder. Flavor with a tablespoonful of vanilla.

Bake in four layers.

FILLING.—Three eggs, with the yolks of the two remaining from the cake, well beaten; one cup of sugar; the juice of two lemons. Cook in vessel set in hot water, on the stove, until it thickens. Stir constantly.

When cold, stir into it a third part of two grated cocoanuts. Spread upon three of the cakes.

FROSTING.—Make a thick, stiff, soft frosting, using a heaping cup of sugar to the white of one egg, and only a half teaspoonful of lemon juice, to whiten it. Flavor with half a teaspoonful of vanilla extract; mix with it a third part of two grated cocoanuts—that is, half of what is left. Spread over the top and sides of the loaf, and, while soft, shower over it the remainder of the cocoanut, insuring its adhering to the cake.

This is the most delicious of all cocoanut cakes. It is a dessert dish properly, to be eaten with a fork.

POUND CAKE.

MRS. FARNSWORTH.

One pound two ounces of butter; one pound sugar; fourteen ounces flour; ten eggs, beaten separately; half teaspoonful mace; one wineglass brandy.

POUND CAKE, No. 2.

MRS. H. W. CLOSSON.

One pound sugar; three-fourths pound butter; one pound flour; ten eggs, beaten separately; one pound raisins, or half pound citron; three-fourths wineglass brandy; ten drops extract of rose; half a nutmeg; grated peel of one lemon. Stir, till very light, the butter and sugar together. Mix the yolks, whites, and flour, alternately. Lastly, add the flavoring and the raisins, dredged with a little of the flour.

WHITE MOUNTAIN CAKE.
ADAPTED BY E. T. J.

One pound sugar; half pound butter; one pound flour; six eggs, beaten separately; two scant teaspoonfuls Royal baking powder, sifted into a little of the flour; one dessertspoonful of vanilla; half teaspoonful extract of lemon, or a very few drops of extract of bitter almond, a few drops of rose, and half a teaspoonful of vanilla; two-thirds cup of milk.

The quantity of flour in this and all cakes, save sponge cake, may require to be slightly varied, owing to the size of the eggs or the quantity of flavoring. The batter should be thin as prudent for baking in jelly cake pans, and may be tested by a small cake. The batter will make two loaves of three cakes each, and may be divided before flavoring. The White Mountain Cake being flavored as directed above, and, when baked, spread with a frosting made in the proportion of one heaping cup of powdered sugar to the white of an egg, and a quarter only of the juice of a lemon, the flavoring to correspond with that of the cake. Spread it as thickly as possible over the cake, and lay the cakes one upon another, frosting the top with slightly stiffer icing.

The other half of the batter may be varied by adding a glass of sherry, a little nutmeg, and ten drops of rose extract, instead of the flavoring used before. This loaf can have jelly between the layers, the top being iced with the frosting used for the first loaf.

If desired, a quarter of a pound of citron, or a half pound of raisins, can be added to the batter just described, and baked in small patty pans.

The loaves can be filled with many other mixtures—with grated orange, made very stiff with sugar, in which case the flavoring of the cake should be a little orange or lemon juice, mixed, with a tiny quantity of the grated peel; or with cocoanut or chocolate.

TUMBLER CAKE.

MRS. BRINCKE.

One large tumbler of butter; one large tumbler sugar; one small tumbler milk; one small tumbler molasses; five tumblers flour; four eggs; one and a half teaspoonfuls soda; one pound raisins; one pound currants; half pound citron; one teaspoonful each of mace, clove, nutmeg, and cinnamon.

FRUIT CAKE.

MRS. THOS. BELKNAP.

Three-fourths pound butter; one pound darkest brown sugar; one pound two ounces browned flour; half pint molasses; half pint milk; one wineglass sherry; four eggs, beaten well; one teaspoonful soda; one tablespoonful cloves; one tablespoonful allspice; two nutmegs.

This receipt will make two loaves of cake, and will keep for weeks.

CINNAMON WAFERS.

MISS FARRAN.

One pound white sugar; quarter pound butter; three eggs; three tablespoonfuls ground cinnamon; one dessertspoonful vanilla extract; one teaspoonful baking powder. Flour only sufficient to roll out thin. Cut into small cakes, with top of a wineglass. When baked, drop a spot of frosting in the middle of each cake. Use to make it whites of two eggs; two cups powdered sugar; ten drops vanilla; a dessertspoonful of lemon juice. The wafers will keep four or five days, but not longer. On losing their freshness, they become powdery and tasteless.

Be careful to obtain the cinnamon from the druggist. If stale, the wafers are ruined.

SAND CAKES.

PLATTSBURG COOK BOOK.

One pound sugar; half pound butter; yolks of two eggs and white of one; one pound flour. Mix the butter and sugar thoroughly, add eggs, well beaten, and flour, alternately. Roll out the cakes thin. Wet the tops with the white of egg, beaten stiff. Sprinkle over them powdered sugar, ground cinnamon, and a few bits blanched almond.

SUGAR CAKES.

JAMAICA, L. I.

Two cups powdered sugar; one cup of butter; four eggs, whites and yolks beaten separately; half a nutmeg, and a little mace; flour enough to roll out soft. Cut in small cakes. Sprinkle granulated sugar on the top.

JACKSON JUMBLES.

MRS. NATHANIEL TERRY.

Three cups sugar; one cup butter; three and a half cups unsifted flour, or five cups sifted flour; one cup sour cream; nutmeg; a little rose water (if extract of rose, ten drops), or vanilla; two eggs.

WATER COOKIES.

MRS. NATHANIEL TERRY.

Three pounds flour; one and a half pounds sugar; three-fourths pound butter; two teaspoonfuls soda, dissolved in a little hot water. Rub the butter into the flour, as if for pastry. Dissolve the sugar in a half pint of boiling water. When cold, wet with this syrup the flour and butter, mixing as if making pastry.

Roll very thin. They will keep some time.

The flavoring can be vanilla, nutmeg, or cinnamon. The receipt makes a large quantity. If properly made, they are crisp and light as pastry, not hard.

MOLASSES GINGERBREAD.

(WITHOUT EGGS.) MISS WOODBRIDGE.

One pint molasses; one cup melted butter; one tablespoonful ginger; one teaspoonful cinnamon; a little nutmeg and clove; one cup cold water. Stir into the molasses a teaspoonful of soda. Beat hard until it foams high. Add the other ingredients, with enough flour to make it stiff. Lastly, add the cupful of water.

GINGERBREAD.

MRS. G. V. N. LOTHROP.

Two cups of molasses; half cup of butter; half cup of brown sugar; one cup of sour milk; a little more than three cups of flour; three-fourths teaspoonful of soda, dissolved in a little water and stirred into the molasses, and three-fourths teaspoonful of soda, dissolved in the milk; two teaspoonfuls ginger.

GINGERBREAD, No. 2.
MEADOW BANK.

Two cups West India molasses; one cup brown sugar; one cup sour milk; half cup butter; one teaspoonful soda; one teaspoonful ginger; a little salt.

Add soda to the milk, which add after the other ingredients have been well stirred together. Use only enough flour to permit the batter to be dropped in cakes.

HARD SUGAR GINGERBREAD.
MRS. NATHANIEL TERRY.

One and a half cups white sugar; two eggs; a piece of butter as large as an egg; one tablespoonful ground ginger; one teaspoonful lemon juice; one teaspoonful soda, dissolved in two tablespoonfuls of milk; flour enough to make a batter which can be rolled out. Roll very thin. Mark in strips, with jagging iron. Sprinkle white sugar on them. Bake a pale brown, in quick oven.

The flour is added after all other ingredients.

GINGER SNAPS.

MRS. NATHANIEL TERRY.

One quart molasses; one pound butter; half pound sugar; one ounce cloves; one cup ginger; one teaspoonful soda; as little flour as can be used to roll out the cakes.

They are very crisp and delicate.

GINGER SNAPS, No. 2.

LYDIA TALBOT.

One and a half cups molasses, West India; one teaspoonful soda. Boil the molasses, stir in the soda, pour it, when boiling hot, over three tablespoonfuls of lard or butter. Add a little salt.

Two tablespoonfuls ginger; half teaspoonful clove; one teaspoonful cinnamon; flour to roll out thin.

PUDDINGS.

APPLE PUDDING.

MISS CORSON.

BUTTER thickly an earthenware pudding mould or bowl with cold butter. Press a layer of bread crumbs, an inch thick, all through the mould, as a lining. Fill the middle with good cooking apples, stewed, mixed with enough sugar to make it moderately sweet; a little nutmeg or grated lemon peel; a tablespoonful of butter, which will melt of itself, when the apple is hot. Add one egg, well beaten. Scatter bread crumbs over the top, and small bits of butter. Bake fifteen minutes, and turn out on a platter.

Eat with Asquam sauce.

BREAD BATTER PUDDING.

MRS. THOS. WAYNE.

Heat a quart of milk, and pour upon two teacups of fine bread crumbs. Beat well, and, when pretty smooth, add half teaspoonful of salt, and, when a little cool, five eggs, beaten separately. Bake, in a buttered dish, until it is set, but not till it separates. Eat with hot liquid sauce.

SOUFFLÉ PUDDING.

MRS. HARRISON.

One tumbler of milk; two heaping tablespoonfuls of flour; quarter pound of butter; two tablespoonfuls of sugar; four eggs. Mix butter, sugar, and flour together. Add the milk, and put in a saucepan over the fire, stirring until it thickens.

Remove from fire, and stir the yolks of the eggs, unbeaten. Beat very hard. Let the mixture cool. Add the whites of the eggs, beaten very light, just before putting into the oven.

Bake twenty minutes, and serve with hot wine sauce.

ORANGE OR LEMON PUDDING.

MRS. A. R. TERRY.

Wet two tablespoonfuls corn starch with a little cold water; when smooth, pour over it a pint and a half of boiling water, as if making starch. When clear and thick, add the yolks of two well-beaten eggs, and the juice of five oranges and one lemon, or four lemons and two oranges, with six heaping tablespoonfuls of sugar. Pour into a dish or mould; when quite stiff, pour over the top a meringue made of the whites of the eggs, beaten with six tablespoonfuls sugar and the juice of half a lemon. Do not allow it to brown, but put in the oven, with doors open, until it sets.

INDIAN PUDDING.

(WITHOUT EGGS.) MISS WOODBRIDGE.

Seven tablespoonfuls Indian meal, stirred into a quart of scalding milk; one cup molasses; butter the size of an egg; one teaspoonful powdered cinnamon; half teaspoonful ginger; one cup cold water, added as the pudding goes into the oven.

Bake three-fourths of an hour.

INDIAN PUDDING, No. 2.

MRS. JUDGE PARKER.

One quart milk, well boiled; half pint corn meal, sprinkled in the milk when hot (have the meal well sifted); half pint molasses; one teaspoonful salt; butter the size of an egg. Mix all thoroughly. Pour over all a pint of cold milk. Stir thoroughly. Put in a buttered baking dish, and bake two hours.

INDIAN PUDDING, No. 3.

MRS. ROSE TERRY COOKE.

Three quarts and one pint sweet milk; three tablespoonfuls (heaped) of ordinary corn meal, *not* granulated; one teacup molasses; one teaspoon salt; half cup butter; ginger to taste. Boil one quart milk, add to it molasses, butter, salt, and spice, and meal stirred smooth with a little cold milk; scald well and then turn into a well-buttered baking dish. When it begins to crust over, stir it all up from the bottom, and add one pint cold milk. Repeat this process every half hour, or oftener if the pudding browns too fast, till the five pints are used, then let it bake till done, six hours at least. Use, when hot, with a sauce of grated or granulated maple sugar, stirred into rich cream, and keep very cold till needed.

This pudding can be reheated indefinitely.

DELMONICO PUDDING.

One quart milk; four even tablespoonfuls corn starch, mixed smooth, with a little cold milk, taken from the quart; the yolks of four eggs, beaten with five tablespoonfuls sugar. When the milk boils, add the corn starch, and stir until quite thick. Take from the fire and add the beaten eggs and sugar. Flavor with one dessertspoonful of vanilla extract. Pour into a pudding dish. Beat the whites of the eggs very light, add three tablespoonfuls sugar, a few drops of vanilla. Spread it over the pudding. Set it in the oven for a few minutes, to set, but not to brown Leave the oven door open.

ENGLISH PLUM PUDDING.

MRS. PECHEN.

One pound suet; half pound flour; two pounds currants; two pounds raisins; one pound citron; half pound sugar; one wineglass of brandy; one wineglass of wine; twelve eggs; one teaspoonful of powdered mace and cloves; one nutmeg; half teaspoonful of salt; quarter pound of orange peel; two tablespoonfuls ginger syrup or brandy peach syrup.

Boil the puddings in small pudding cloths, holding about a quart each, five hours, not letting it stop boiling one moment.

These will last an indefinite length of time. Hang in a cool, dry place. When used, plunge in boiling water, and boil one hour.

PLUM PUDDING.

MRS. MCHARG.

One cup suet, chopped fine; one cup molasses; one cup chopped apple; one cup milk; one small teaspoonful of salt; one teaspoonful each of cinnamon, allspice, mace, cloves, nutmeg; two cups chopped raisins, more if you like; one cup dried currants; half pound citron.

If liked, add quarter pound of candied orange peel,

and half a pound of almonds, blanched and slit, with a penknife, in four parts.

Two well-beaten eggs (if eggs are plentiful, use four); two cups of flour.

Boil three hours, and serve with hot liquid sauce.

PLUM PUDDING, No. 2.

MISS CHARLOTTE ELY.

One pound fruit cake; one teacup suet; one heaping cup of flour; three-fourths glass of wine; one teaspoonful powdered cinnamon; four eggs, beaten separately; half teacup milk; one nutmeg.

Boil four hours.

RICE PUDDING.

MRS. A. M. DIAZ.

One-third cup rice. Let it swell in a quart of milk, in a farina kettle, on the back of the stove, until quite thick. Then add another pint of milk, three tablespoonfuls sugar.

Put in a pudding dish, cover it closely. While baking, stir the pudding now and then. When nearly done, remove the cover. Bake only until set, taking care not to allow it to separate.

GRAHAM PUDDING.

MRS. JUDGE PARKER.

One cup of molasses ; one cup of tepid water ; two cups of graham flour ; one cup of chopped raisins ; one teaspoonful soda. Steam three hours. Eat with golden sauce.

GRAHAM PUDDING, No. 2.

MISS PARLOA.

One and a half cups graham flour ; one cup milk ; half cup molasses ; one cup chopped raisins ; one teaspoonful soda ; half teaspoonful salt.

Dissolve soda in a spoonful of the milk. Add the rest of milk to the molasses, pour over flour, and, lastly, add raisins. Boil, in mould, four hours.

SAGO AND APPLE PUDDING.

ELIZABETH COPPET.

Soak six tablespoonfuls of sago or tapioca in a pint of warm water. Pare six sour apples, and core them. Butter a dish, place the apples in it, and fill the cores with sugar and a little grated nutmeg. Melt a small cup of sugar in the sago and water, pour two-thirds of the mixture over the apples, and put in the oven. When it has slowly baked an hour, pour in the rest of the sago, stirring occasionally, and pressing the apples down.

SAGO AND APPLE PUDDING, No. 2.
ANNIE CONOLLEY.

Soak six tablespoonfuls of sago or tapioca in a quart of warm water, on the back of the stove. Pare, core, and cut in eighths six greening or Baldwin apples. Butter a pudding dish, put in the apples. Slightly sweeten the sago and water, and grate in a third of a nutmeg. Pour over the apples. Put it in the oven, with a plate over the top ; remove it ten minutes before it is done. Stir it, gently, from time to time.

Eat warm, not hot, with sweetened cream, or, what is best of all, half a pint of cream, whipped with egg-beater, with a tablespoonful of powdered sugar.

CHOCOLATE PUDDING.
MRS. B. F. D. ADAMS.

One cup of chocolate, dissolved in a little hot milk. Add to it a pint of milk, boiling hot ; the yolks of two eggs, beaten with a cup of sugar ; a tablespoonful of corn starch, dissolved in a very little cold milk, and the melted chocolate. Let it thicken, in a double boiler, on the stove. Pour into a pudding dish, and, when cool, spread over the top a meringue, made of the whites of three eggs and three tablespoonfuls sugar. Put it in the oven, with open doors, to set.

SPONGE CAKE PUDDING.

FROM BOSTON.

A quarter cup of sugar; a half cup of flour; a quarter cup of butter; five eggs; one pint of milk, boiled.

Mix flour and sugar. Wet with a little cold milk. Stir into the boiling milk. Cook until smooth. Add the butter, the well-beaten yolks of the eggs, then the beaten whites. Pour into a buttered dish. Set into a pan of boiling water, and bake, in a moderate oven, forty minutes. Eat hot, with a liquid sauce.

STEAMED PUDDING.

E. T. J.

A quarter tumbler of butter; a half tumbler of sugar; a half tumbler of milk; a half tumbler of molasses; two and a half tumblers of flour; two eggs; one large tumbler of fruit; three-fourths teaspoonful of soda; one teaspoonful each of clove, cinnamon, and mace or nutmeg.

Steam three hours. Eat with liquid sauce.

TAPIOCA PUDDING.

MRS. NATHANIEL TERRY.

Soak four ounces of tapioca (the large tapioca is best), in a quart of milk, for several hours, until quite soft. Let it boil a few minutes; if quite thick, add a little milk. When cold, add four eggs, beaten separately; four ounces of sugar; a glass of wine; the peel of a lemon, grated, and, lastly, a pint of cream. This will make two puddings.

Orange flower water may be substituted for the lemon and wine.

The following receipt is an improvement on the one above given, being more delicate. Both rules require very careful baking, since the cream-like consistence is to be secured.

TAPIOCA PUDDING, No. 2.

ADAPTED BY E. T. J.

Soak four tablespoonfuls tapioca, in a quart of milk, one hour; then add one pint of milk, and cook slowly in double boiler, until the tapioca is thoroughly done and soft. Pour into a large dish, add another pint of cold milk, a pint of cream, a half teaspoonful salt, five well-beaten eggs, the grated rind of a lemon, a dessertspoonful of vanilla extract, eight drops of rose water, a wineglass of wine, stirred into ten large tablespoonfuls of sugar.

This will make three puddings. Butter the dishes, set them in a dripping pan, pour hot water around them, and replenish as it boils away. Be very careful not to cook too long. The pudding is like thick cream, when properly baked.

PRUNE PUDDING.

MRS. WATSON WEBB.

Stew, gently, a pound of French prunes in a pint of water. When nearly soft, add a teacup and a half of sugar. When quite done, remove the stones, and cut each prune into four pieces. Have a scant quarter box of Nelson's gelatine, dissolved in a gill of boiling water, on the stove. Strain it into the prunes. Add two tablespoonfuls of brandy, pour into a mould, and set on ice. Serve with whipped cream. A border mould may be used, with a hollow in the center, in which the whipped cream can be piled up. A little lemon juice and grated peel improves it. Canned peaches and apricots are very nice prepared with gelatine in a similar way, adding a little lemon juice and either cutting the fruit in bits, or straining it after slowly stewing with more sugar.

GOLDEN SAUCE.

MRS. JUDGE PARKER.

One cup of butter and one cup of sugar, well beaten together; a little nutmeg, or the grated peel and juice of a lemon. Add four tablespoonfuls hot water, then the beaten yolk and afterwards the beaten white of one egg. Beat well.

Put the sauce into the boat and set it in a saucepan of hot water. Stir gently from time to time.

This receipt does not differ essentially from Miss Parloa's golden sauce, except that only a third of a cup of butter is used, and two tablespoonfuls of wine are substituted for the lemon and water.

It is especially used for graham pudding.

SAUCE FOR APPLE PUDDING.

PLATTSBURG COOK BOOK.

Beat one egg very light. Stir into it a cup of white sugar. Then add four tablespoonfuls boiling milk, and add, lastly, the grated rind of a lemon. This is smooth and foamy, and serves well hot for apple puddings or meringues, or for any pudding or blanc mange usually eaten with cream.

The flavoring can be varied, but lemon peel is best to eat with apple pudding.

LIQUID PUDDING SAUCE.
SARAH LAUGHLIN.

Beat together half a cup of butter and a cup of sugar. Add a little nutmeg. Heat, very hot, a wineglass of wine or a half glass of brandy. Beat it into the sauce, which will foam throughout.

LIQUID PUDDING SAUCE, No. 2.
MAGGIE M.

One cup butter; two cups sugar, powdered. Stir to a cream, then drop in a piece of ice, and beat hard. Add half a cup of brandy, which has been chilled on ice, a teaspoonful at a time. If not sufficiently thin, add a little iced milk. Transfer to sauce boat, set in a saucepan of cold water. Set on the fire. Let it boil twenty minutes. Serve in sauce boat. Add a little grated nutmeg to the butter and sugar.

LIQUID PUDDING SAUCE, No. 3.
MARION HARLAND.

One and a quarter cups powdered sugar; one quarter cup of butter; one quarter cup boiling water. Measure the water, and keep on the stove or spirit lamp. Stir the butter and sugar together; wet from time to time with half a teaspoonful of the hot water, beating hard. If more water is used, the butter is melted and the sauce is ruined. When all the water is added, the mixture should be a foamy mass.

Add half a wineglass of brandy, a little at a time, and a quarter of a grated nutmeg. Pour the mixture into a sauce boat, set it into a saucepan of boiling water, and stir occasionally. When hot, remove to back of stove, still in the water, until it is needed.

PIES.

BEST PASTRY.

MRS. NATHANIEL TERRY.

MEASURE one quart sifted pastry flour. Place a handful of it upon the moulding board. Have a coffeecupful of butter and one of best lard, made very cold, either by keeping for half an hour upon ice, or by packing it in a pan of snow. Roll out the butter in the flour, upon the moulding board, into thin sheets, place it on tin pans, and set them upon the ice or snow until wanted for use.

Scrape into the flour in the dish the butter that may have crumbled on the board, with the remaining flour. Add a small teaspoonful of salt. Cut up the lard, in the flour, with a knife, or rub it with the tips of your fingers, quickly and lightly, until it is all a granulated mass. Wet it with three-fourths of a coffeecup of ice water, stirring it with a knife. Take a little sifted flour, not a portion of the original quart, sift a little on the board, turn out the dough upon it, flour the rolling pin, roll the pastry lightly to a square mass, an inch thick and a foot square. Place a layer of the rolled butter on the dough, not extending within two inches of the edge on any side. Fold over the side edges, then the top edges, not meeting on any side. Double the dough, turn it, and roll again, as before, until the supply of butter is exhausted. The measure given will make three layers. When doubled together for the last time, cut off a piece from the roll, sufficient for the bottom crust of the first pie. Roll it a quarter of an inch thick, cover with it a pie plate, which has been well buttered, trimming off the edges with a sharp, well-floured knife. Fill the plate with fruit or mince meat, or whatever filling you have prepared. Roll out the top crust slightly thicker than the bottom. When trimmed off, cut a slit in center of crust. Cut the edge of the paste with the knife at every inch; this will secure the edges of the crust, but not injure its consistency. Bake in a hot oven, and watch carefully. It is better only lightly brown, but thoroughly risen and well cooked.

For berry or small fruit pies, use a soup plate, or any deep plate with a rim.

Pie plates, as well as cake tins, should be buttered with cold butter, melted butter running off.

Although the cook books recommend chilling the pastry over some three different periods, of twenty minutes each, it is found, by having the shortening very hard to begin with, using ice water to wet it, and manipulating the dough as quickly and lightly as possible, that the handsomest puff paste can be made. Dexterity is the main thing which can be relied on, and which practice will certainly teach. In summer, it is, of course, better, if the butter seems soft, to place the dough for as long a time as possible on the ice. I have never found it necessary to wet the strip of paste around the edge of the pie.

All butter can be used, if preferred, but the pastry will not be so handsome. Do not use more than a saltspoonful of salt, if no lard is used.

This receipt, if closely followed, will make the handsomest puff paste.

APPLE PIE.

Slice five sour apples very thin. Line a pie plate with crust, made after the puff paste receipt, but using a little less shortening, and rolling it out in flour, not included in the quart mentioned. Roll the under crust thin.

Fill the plate with the apples. Cover it with paste, rolled somewhat thicker. Cut two slits in the middle. When baked, remove with care the top crust, lay on a plate. Stir the apple lightly. Stir in a heaping teaspoonful of butter, half a grated nutmeg, and enough sugar to make it palatable. Replace the top crust. This method is so superior to the mode of preparing the apple before cooking that it is worth the trial.

MINCE PIE.

ADAPTED BY E. T. J.

Two pounds boiled tongue, not smoked (Richardson & Robbins' jellied tongues are the best), chopped fine; one pound suet, with strings removed, and also chopped fine; three pounds brown sugar; four pounds tart apples, chopped fine; one pound currant jelly, or cherry jam, damson or any sub-acid sweetmeat will do; two pounds of raisins, chopped coarsely; one pound Sultana raisins, stemmed and whole; half pound candied orange and lemon peel, shredded fine; one and a quarter pounds of citron, cut fine; grated peel and juice of two lemons; two nutmegs; one teaspoonful powdered clove; one teaspoonful powdered cinnamon; one teaspoonful salt; one teaspoonful extract of rose; one pint sherry; half pint of brandy; half pint cider.

If desired, when made into pies, some whole raisins and larger bits of citron can be scattered over the mince meat.

If too thin, add either syrup of sweetmeats or a little more sherry or cider.

Do not cook it at all before making into pies. Keep in a stone jar, in a cool, dry place, with a piece of white paper laid over it, and a cloth tied over the mouth of jar.

MINCE MEAT, No. 2.

MRS. H. W. CLOSSON.

One large boiled tongue, carefully trimmed and chopped fine, or a two-pound whole tongue of Richardson & Robbins'; four pounds of chopped apples; one pint of cider; one quart of brandy; three pounds brown sugar; three pounds chopped raisins; one pound citron, cut fine; nutmeg, cinnamon, and mace to taste; the rind and juice of a lemon; one tablespoonful of vanilla extract.

MINCE MEAT, No. 3.

MRS. A. R. TERRY.

Two pounds raisins; one pound currants; one pound suet; two pounds chopped apples; two and a half pounds sugar; three lemons, juice and grated peel; two ounces cinnamon; two nutmegs; a little clove; one pint of neutral spirit. Wet with sherry.

RISSOLES À LA CRÊME.

MRS. HENDERSON.

Prepare the paste and proceed as directed in the previously given receipt.

Prepare the filling as follows: Boil a pint of milk in a double boiler. When boiling, add a tablespoonful of flour and two tablespoonfuls corn starch, wet and rubbed smooth, in a little cold milk. Stir the milk until it thickens, take from the stove, add three well-beaten eggs, six tablespoonfuls sugar. Return to fire for a moment. Flavor with a dessertspoonful of vanilla, six drops rose water, and the grated peel of a lemon. Pour upon a platter to harden. Cut a square for the rissoles, or, if soft, a teaspoonful for each one.

The rissoles are very nice with any thick jam for the filling. The shape of the rissoles is like a crescent.

BAKED APPLE DUMPLINGS.

MRS. THOS. WAYNE.

Make some ordinary pie crust, using the rule given for puff paste, deducting a quarter of that amount of butter.

Roll out thin, cut in square pieces, and enclose an apple, pared and cored, in each, wrapping the crust about it and pinching it tightly, to close it.

Place in a pudding dish, buttered, to bake. When the crust is a delicate brown, baste the dumplings with a bowlful of sauce, made by stirring together a tablespoonful of butter, a teacup of white sugar, and a pint of hot water. Baste from time to time, letting the apples remain five minutes in the oven after the last basting. If possible, serve in the same dish. The dumplings will be glazed, and a little thick syrup be in the dish. It needs no other sauce.

CREAMS AND JELLIES.

GENERAL REMARKS.

NELSON'S gelatine is preferable to any other, one-quarter box being equal to one-third box of Cox's.

All preparations with gelatine, having white of egg, beaten stiff, or whipped cream, added, should be placed on ice, or in a double vessel, having snow or cracked ice in the lower part, and carefully watched. When the congealing has begun, add, instantly, the cream or eggs, as it becomes stiff at once, and then no stirring will amalgamate the materials. Stir the cream very lightly in with a fork, and at once pour into moulds. The long process formerly necessary in making snow pudding is thus avoided, and the result quite as successful.

WHIPPED CREAM.

Cream whipped with the Dover egg beater is far better than that made by means of the old syllabub pump. It requires only five minutes' brisk turning, for the whole mass to become stiff, more compact than the stiffest beaten white of egg. It will remain so for several days.

For use as sauce, or to eat with sweetmeats, add only a tablespoonful of sugar, powdered, to the cream.

A half pint of cream, whipped, makes the best possible sauce for any cold pudding.

Cream for whipping should be twenty-four hours' old, and uniformly thick, as lumpy cream will turn to butter. It is needful to use a little sugar, to prevent the same result.

When cream is not abundant, the following receipt can be used for a quart of whip.

WHIPPED CREAM, No. 2.

MRS. JAMES BIDDLE.

One pint sweetened cream; one tablespoonful vanilla extract; two tablepoonfuls wine, sherry; the beaten whites of three eggs. Beat with Dover egg beater.

SPANISH CREAM.

ADAPTED BY E. T. J.

One quart of milk; one-quarter box of Nelson's gelatine; five tablespoonfuls sugar; five eggs. Put the milk into a double boiler, beat the yolks of the eggs with the sugar. When the milk boils, remove from fire. Stir in the egg and sugar, return to the fire, and stir until it thickens. It will not be very thick. Meanwhile dissolve the gelatine in a little hot water, on the stove, letting it boil up once. Stir it into the custard and set it on the ice or fill the bottom part of the double boiler with ice or snow. When cool, but not stiff, stir in the flavoring — a tablespoonful of sherry, mixed with the same quantity of sugar, a dessertspoonful of vanilla, and five drops of extract of rose.

When the custard is stiff enough to hold the spoon, stir in lightly, with a fork, the beaten whites of the five eggs, being careful to add them at once, upon the mixture becoming thick, as it hardens almost immediately, and if at all too stiff, the cream will be ruined. Fill the cups or moulds, and turn out on a dish when quite set.

COFFEE JELLY.

MRS. A. B. ADAMS.

Allow a quarter box of Nelson's gelatine to soak an hour in a half pint of cold coffee. Then heat a pint and a half of made coffee; add three tablespoonfuls of sugar, and pour it over the soaked gelatine. Put in moulds, rinsed in cold water, and set on ice. Eat with cream and sugar, or whipped cream.

CHARLOTTE RUSSE.

MRS. C. W. GRANT.

Make a rich custard, with a half a pint of milk, three eggs, and eight tablespoonfuls sugar. When still hot, add one-third box of Nelson or Cox's gelatine, which, dissolved in a little water, has boiled up once on the stove. Over a spirit lamp, it will boil in one moment. It should be stirred constantly, and will be found dissolved thoroughly. Stir it gradually into the custard. Fill the lower part of the double boiler in which the custard was made with snow or pounded ice, and set in a cold place. This will thicken so quickly that you will have barely time to prepare the other ingredients before the custard is congealed. Flavor a quart of cream with a tablespoonful of sugar, and whip stiff with a Dover egg-beater. Line the sides and bottom of two oval or oblong pans with lady fingers, or strips of sponge cake, two inches wide, from which the crust is removed. By this time the custard will probably be about as stiff as boiled oatmeal. Flavor with half a wineglass of sherry, five drops of rose water, and a dessertspoonful of vanilla extract. Put a spoonful of sugar into the wine before stirring it into the custard. Quickly add the whipped cream, because the mixture hardens very rapidly when it begins to thicken. Stir in gently, but thoroughly, with a fork, taking care to reach the bottom. If the custard is found to be quite stiff, it should be set into boiling water and beaten hard until it softens, as it will be ruined should the cream and custard not thoroughly mix. Fill the pans and set in a cold place. It will easily turn out upon a dish, by running a knife between the cake and the pan, inverting the pan upon a dish and tapping the bottom with the knife handle.

If only a pint of cream can be obtained, the charlotte will still be very nice, but will fill only one pan. Should the snow or ice melt before the mixture is hard, replenish it.

This is the best receipt for charlotte russe known.

CHARLOTTE RUSSE, No. 2.

MRS. JAMES BIDDLE.

One-third box gelatine in a half pint of new milk. Soak for an hour and then dissolve, by setting the bowl in a pail of hot water on the stove. Stir the yolks of four eggs into three pints of cream, sweetened and flavored with vanilla. Stir in the gelatine. When it begins to stiffen, add the well-beaten whites of four eggs. Line the mould with sponge cake. When the mixture is stiff, pour in mould.

CHARLOTTE RUSSE, No. 3.

(WITH LITTLE OR NO CREAM.) E. T. J.

One quart milk; five eggs; eight tablespoonfuls of sugar. Put the milk in a double boiler, beat the yolks of the eggs with the sugar. When the milk boils, stir in the eggs and sugar. Stir until the custard thickens.

Pour a little water upon a third of a box of Nelson or Cox's gelatine. Let it boil up once, and stir gradually into the custard. Flavor with a half glass of sherry, sweetened; five drops of rose water, and a dessertspoonful of vanilla cream.

Put some snow or ice into the lower part of the double boiler. Set the custard into the refrigerator. When it begins to thicken, beat the whites of the eggs; stir gently into the stiffened custard. If you have a little cream, add it to the custard before the eggs.

Line a mould with lady-fingers, or strips of sponge cake; pour in the custard. It will be found an excellent substitute for charlotte russe made of cream.

MILK BLANC MANGE.

E. T. J.

Blanc mange can be made palatable with little cream, although not so good as when no milk is used.

Take a third of a box of Nelson's gelatine to a quart of milk. Cover the gelatine with half a pint of the milk; let it stand an hour. Heat the milk to boiling point, adding to it a little stick cinnamon, broken up. Pour the hot milk, through a strainer, over the gelatine. When thoroughly dissolved, sweeten the milk, add a half teaspoonful of vanilla, and pour into moulds previously rinsed with cold water. If you have a little cream, stir it gently into the milk, when it is slightly thick. If put in at first, the cream will rise to the top. Care must be taken not to let the milk first become stiff.

CREAM BLANC MANGE.

MRS. ROSE TERRY COOKE.

Pour half a pint of milk upon a fourth of a box of Nelson's gelatine. Let it stand an hour. Heat a pint of milk, boiling with it a few bits of stick cinnamon. Pour the hot milk over the gelatine; stir until it dissolves. Add six tablespoonfuls of sugar, a pint of cream, a teaspoonful of vanilla extract, and a half saltspoonful of salt. Pour into moulds, which have been rinsed with cold water.

CHOCOLATE BLANC MANGE.

MRS. JAMES BIDDLE.

Grate one and a half cakes of Baker's chocolate (*i. e.*, of the three divisions of a half-pound cake of Baker's chocolate, take one and one-half); add a little boiling water, and stir on the fire until it looks smooth and glossy. Melt a quarter box of Nelson's gelatine. Boil a pint and a half of milk. When boiling, stir in the chocolate. Add five large tablespoonfuls of sugar. Remove from fire; add the melted gelatine. Flavor with a dessertspoonful of vanilla.

Pour into moulds, which have been rinsed in cold water.

COFFEE CREAM.

ADAPTED FROM C. E. OWEN BY E. T. J.

Make a custard of half a pint of milk, two eggs, and four tablespoonfuls sugar. Dissolve a quarter box of Nelson's gelatine in a gill of water, on the stove. Let it boil up once, and strain into the warm custard. Add a gill of very strong coffee, freshly made. Set on the ice, and when stiffening, stir in lightly a pint of whipped cream.

Use a fork for mixing. Put in a mould, and eat with cream.

This cream can be prepared by melting the gelatine

in a little hot water, adding a half pint of strong made coffee and a half pint of hot milk. When cool and stiffening, stir in a pint of cream, whipped.

STRAWBERRY CREAM.

ADAPTED FROM C. E. OWEN, BY E. T. J.

Put half a pint of ripe strawberries, or raspberries, through a sieve. Make the fruit very sweet. Dissolve half an ounce of gelatine in a saucepan, with two tablespoonfuls of cold water, and the juice of a lemon. Let it slowly melt. Strain the gelatine into the fruit. Set on the ice, and when stiffening, add half a pint of cream, whipped with a Dover egg beater. Put in a mould. This makes about a pint and a half of the cream.

JELLIED FRUIT.

ADAPTED FROM CATHARINE OWEN BY E. T. J.

Dissolve one-third box of Nelson's gelatine in a gill of water. Squeeze the juice from a quart of raspberries, strawberries, currants, or blackberries. Add the juice of a lemon. Make very sweet. Warm slightly. Stir in the gelatine. Set on ice. When beginning to stiffen, stir in lightly a pint of whipped cream. Pour into a mould. If you can get no cream, add in its place the whites of three eggs, whipped very light.

JELLIED FRUIT, No. 2.

ADAPTED BY E. T. J.

Dissolve a third box of Nelson's gelatine in a gill of water, on the stove. Rub a quart of raspberries or strawberries through a fine sieve, first passing them through a potato strainer, to break the fruit. Make it very sweet. Add the juice of a lemon. Warm slightly. Stir in the gelatine. Set on the ice. When becoming stiff, stir in a pint of whipped cream, or the beaten whites of three eggs. Pour in a mould. If eggs are used, the charlotte should be eaten with a little cream.

This preparation can be made with other fruits, such as perfectly ripe peaches, pine apple, grated, or with bananas.

It is better, however, made from small fruits, which are juicy. Great care should be taken to make the fruit pulp sweet enough not to curdle the cream.

ORANGE JELLY.

ADAPTED BY E. T. J.

The juice of four oranges and two lemons should be used for a quart of jelly. Take a third of a package of Nelson's gelatine (a fourth will do in cold weather), pour over it a half pint of water, let it stand an hour. The grated peel of one lemon and one orange may be added then to the gelatine. Pour over it, when soaked an hour, a pint and a half of boiling water; stir till dissolved. Make the jelly quite sweet. Add the juice of the lemons and oranges. The prettiest way of serving is to scrape carefully away the pulp of a sufficient number of oranges, eight probably going to a quart of jelly; set them up in a pan of Indian meal, fill them with the liquid jelly, nearly full. If carefully done, the color of the jelly makes the dish a very pretty one.

WINE JELLY.

E. T. J.

The ordinary long process of making wine jelly is to be found in all the books of receipts. With great care, the making can be rendered much more simple.

Put the package of Nelson's gelatine on the stove, in a small saucepan, with half a pint of hot water. Watch it carefully and stir constantly; in a minute it will boil up and thoroughly dissolve. Meanwhile have boiling two quarts of water. Pour it over four sticks of cinnamon, broken up, and the grated peel of two lemons. Add the dissolved gelatine, stirring well; a pint of sherry or Rhine wine; the juice of three lemons, and, if desired, of one orange. Make the jelly very sweet, adding, last of all, a wineglass of brandy. Strain through a muslin cloth, laid on a hair sieve, into moulds, and set on ice. If set in ice water, or in water often changed, the jelly will become firm in three-quarters of an hour, the whole process taking only an hour.

SWEET CIDER JELLY.

MRS. HENRY ABBEY.

Soak a package of gelatine in half a pint of cold water for an hour. Meanwhile let two quarts of sweet cider be poured over the peel of two lemons and a few sticks of cinnamon, broken up. Strain out the lemon and cinnamon, after an hour's soaking. Pour a quart of boiling water over the gelatine, and stir until dissolved.

Add the cider and the juice of three lemons. Make the liquid quite sweet. Strain and set away in moulds. A little more cinnamon may be used than for wine jelly, and a glass of brandy, if desired.

APPLE MERINGUE.

MRS. GEO. BRINLEY.

Pare and quarter six large apples (greenings or king apples are best). Make a syrup of a pint of boiling water and a large teacup of white sugar. When boiling, drop in a third of the apples; let them cook until clear, but not broken. Remove them to a pudding dish, draining the syrup back into the saucepan. Drop half the remaining apples into the syrup. When all are cooked, the syrup will probably be thick enough to pour over the apple in the dish. If not, allow it to cook a few moments longer, taking care that it does not burn.

Make a meringue of the whites of three eggs and twelve tablespoonfuls of powdered sugar. Beat the eggs light, add the sugar, half the juice of a lemon, three drops of extract of rose. Spread the meringue over the apple; set it in a cool oven, and leave the door open, while the meringue slowly dries. It should be in the oven twenty minutes.

Eat with cream.

The flavoring of the meringue can be varied, if desired, but nothing should be added to the cooked apples, provided the apples are fine.

The dish should be eaten cold.

SNOWS.

LEMON OR ORANGE SNOW.

THE juice of three or four large lemons, the grated peel of two; whites of four eggs, beaten stiff; a quarter box of Nelson's gelatine; one cup of cold water; one pint boiling water; one large wineglass sherry; a half teaspoonful nutmeg; two cups powdered sugar.

Pour the cup of cold water over the gelatine. Add lemon juice, peel, nutmeg, and sugar. Cover and let it stand an hour.

Pour over this the boiling water, and, when dissolved, add the wine. Set on ice. When as stiff as oatmeal porridge, add the whites of eggs, stirring in lightly with a fork. Put in an oblong mould and set on ice. Serve on a platter, with a bit of laced paper under the form, which, when turned out, looks like a block of ice, or frozen snow. Eat with cream and sugar, or with a little whipped cream.

Orange snow can be made in the same way, using four oranges and one lemon.

PINEAPPLE SNOW.

ADAPTED BY E. T. J.

Grate a fresh pineapple, or take a can of pineapple put up by a reliable maker. If the latter is used, the pineapple should be chopped fine and stewed tender.

Soak a quarter box of Nelson's gelatine in half a pint of cold water, for an hour. Measure the pineapple, and if there is a pint, take only half a pint of boiling water to pour over the gelatine. If less than a pint of pineapple, make up the quantity by hot water. Pour it over the soaked gelatine, stir till dissolved, add two cups of sugar, the grated pineapple, a glass of sherry. If desired, the liquid can be strained to extract the grated pineapple, and where canned chopped pineapple is used, it is necessary to strain it out. With the grated fresh pineapple it is better left in. Set on ice. When nearly stiff, add the whites, well beaten, of four eggs.

Put in a mould, as with lemon snow. Turn out and eat with cream.

CREAM SNOW.

E. T. J.

Soak a quarter box of Nelson's gelatine in half a pint of milk one hour. Heat a pint and a half of cream; pour on the soaked gelatine till dissolved. Add a cup and a half of sugar, two tablespoonfuls of rum, or a dessertspoonful of vanilla, six drops of rose, and ten drops of almond, or any flavor. Set on ice. When nearly stiff, stir in the whites of four eggs, beaten stiff. Pour in mould, and, when stiff, turn out on dish.

APPLE SNOW.

MRS. A. B. ADAMS.

Beat, very light, the whites of two eggs. Stew and make very sweet three fine apples. Strain through a sieve or fine strainer. Flavor with the grated peel of a lemon and three drops of extract of rose. Beat, a spoonful at a time, the strained and sweetened apple into the white of egg. If carefully done, the mixture will hold all the apple. Beat it, with a Dover egg-beater, in the bowl in which it goes to table. Eat with cream.

ICES AND ICE CREAMS.

ICE CREAM, WITH LITTLE CREAM.

E. T. J.

BOIL one quart of milk in double boiler. Beat five eggs, separately. Add to the yolks ten tablespoonfuls sugar. When the milk boils, pour it over the yolks and sugar, beating hard. Then quickly pour the whole over the beaten whites, and return at once to the fire. Stir gently, now and then, until the mass thickens. It will be foamy to the bottom of the boiler, if carefully made.

When thick, remove from stove and set in a cold place. When quite cold, add what cream you can get, a pint if possible, a half pint will do. Flavor the cream with a tablespoonful of vanilla extract. Stir gently into the custard, which should not have one drop of liquid remaining, but be all like beaten cream.

Freeze in patent freezer. If a pint of cream is used, this receipt will make nearly a gallon of ice cream. It is as much custard as can properly be put into a gallon freezer. It is the best substitute for ice cream made entirely of cream, known to cookery.

Cream for freezing should never, in summer, stand over twelve hours; in winter, it may be left twenty-four hours. Any suspicion of want of freshness should cause the rejection of cream for freezing. Some chemical change, as yet not understood, but which has been proved dangerous, takes place in the process of freezing.

VANILLA ICE CREAM.

Make very sweet two quarts and a pint of sweet cream, using ten tablespoonfuls of sugar, granulated, with a large tablespoonful of vanilla extract, or the grated rind of a lemon, for flavoring.

This quantity will nearly fill, when frozen in the Star or any other first-class patent freezer, a gallon can.

The cream may be varied, by using less flavoring and serving with crystalized apricots, chopped, and put on the same plate.

Crystalized apricots, plums, peaches, cherries, or any fruit, except pears, limes, and small green oranges, may be chopped and added to the cream, when frozen, before repacking.

Ripe strawberries, well sugared and firm, may be lightly stirred into the cream when frozen.

LEMON ICE CREAM.

ADAPTED BY E. T. J.

To a quart of cream add the grated rind of one fine lemon, and sweeten it sufficiently. When frozen and ready to repack, stir into the cream the juice of the lemon, made thick with sugar, If the cream is perfectly sweet, this will not curdle it.

ORANGE ICE CREAM.

ADAPTED BY E. T. J.

To a quart of cream, made very sweet, add, when frozen and ready to repack, the juice of two oranges, made stiff with sugar. It can be thoroughly mixed, by turning the dasher several times. Small bits of fresh orange, free from skin and membrane, can be stirred into it at same time.

BANANA ICE CREAM.

MRS. JOHN WHITE.

Make ice cream as in receipt on page 97, and when frozen, add a dozen ripe bananas, peeled and sliced. Stir in gently and pack in mould. The vanilla flavoring may be omitted, and a glass of well-sweetened sherry stirred in just before freezing.

Another method is to grate ten ripe bananas, mix them with three pints of rather thin cream. Sweeten well and freeze. Some fresh sliced banana can be stirred in before the cream is repacked.

BRANDY-PEACH ICE CREAM.

MRS. JOHN F. MINES.

Pour off part of the syrup from a can of peaches. Pour over them enough brandy to thoroughly flavor them. Let them stand several hours. Chop the peaches fine. Add a quart of cream, first sweetening the peaches, and freeze.

PEACH ICE CREAM.

E. T. J.

This is one of the most delicious of all frozen dishes.

Rub a dozen or fifteen ripe peaches, pared and stoned, through a sieve. Make it very sweet. Add an equal quantity of sweet cream, measured, and freeze.

STRAWBERRY ICE CREAM.

E. T. J.

Rub one quart of perfectly ripe strawberries through a hair sieve. With some care, the fruit will all pass through, leaving the seeds in the sieve. Make the strawberry pulp very sweet, using about a pound and a half of sugar. Add to this a quart of cream, which need not be very thick, and freeze. A pint of rich cream can be diluted with a pint of milk. This quantity, when frozen, will yield over three quarts of ice.

It is one of the most delicious ices known to the chef's art.

If the mixture is very thick, a pint of milk can still be added.

The substance of the frozen cream is of velvet softness.

APRICOT ICE CREAM.

E. T. J.

This cream is made as in the preceding receipt, using ripe apricots, instead of peaches.

If ripe, fresh apricots cannot be obtained, the large California apricots, in cans, put up by the Golden Gate Packing Company, can be used, discarding the juice, and rubbing the fruit only through the sieve. Canned peaches, for some unexplained reason, cannot be used in this way. They have a peculiar, tin flavor, which is strongly developed in freezing.

CHOCOLATE ICE CREAM.

Make a custard as in the receipt for ice cream, given on page 97. Melt a quarter of a pound of Baker's chocolate in a little water, scraping the chocolate fine and stirring it on the stove until it has boiled two or three minutes and is quite smooth. Add the cream, a pint or less, to the melted chocolate. When the custard is quite cold, add the cream and chocolate with a tablespoonful of vanilla extract, and freeze.

COFFEE ICE CREAM.

Prepare the custard as in receipt on page 97. Add to a pint of cream a pint of strong, clear coffee, well sweetened. Mix with the custard, when cold, and freeze.

BISCUIT ICE CREAM.

Grate ten Naples or sponge biscuit, the square cakes made by confectioners, which are dry. Make a custard, as in receipt first given. Add the grated sponge cakes to the sweetened and flavored cream, and freeze.

A still better way is to take two quarts and a pint of sweet cream, sweeten with eight tablespoonfuls of sugar, and flavor with a tablespoonful of vanilla extract. Add the grated sponge cake, and freeze.

ICES.

The old method of making ices is so inferior to that where the body of the fruit, rubbed through a sieve, is used, that no receipts, save for the latter, are given, except for lemon or orange ices. In preparing these ices, great care must be taken to sweeten the fruit thoroughly, as it is said to lose this quality in freezing. These fruit ices, which I have called "frozen fruits," are of the consistence of the most velvety ice cream, and can be made of almost any fruit which is ripe and juicy. The color of the ices is beautiful, especially of the raspberry.

LEMON ICE.

E. T. J.

For a gallon of ice, take the juice of eight fine lemons and four oranges. Add two pounds of granulated sugar, and two quarts and a pint of water. Just before putting into the freezer, add the whites of five well-beaten eggs.

ORANGE ICE.

E. T. J.

Peel ten fine oranges, remove all the white skin, and rub through a fruit strainer (the new mashers, which are used for preparing potatoes à la neige, will do for this purpose, but in that case the oranges must be first cut into bits). Add to the orange the juice of three lemons, and a pound and a half of sugar. If the fruit is sour, more sugar may be required. If you have a little of the sweet preserved orange, it is very nice, added after the ice is frozen, before repacking. It should be chopped very fine.

FROZEN FRUIT ICES.

FROZEN STRAWBERRIES.

MRS. JOHN C. WHITE.

STRAIN three pints or two quarts of fine ripe, fresh strawberries through a hair sieve. It is better to first mash the fruit with a silver spoon; cover it with a pound of granulated sugar, and let it stand several hours before straining.

Add to the strained fruit the juice of one fine lemon, two pounds of sugar; but if one pound was previously used over the bruised fruit, add now only one pound more; three pints of cold water, and freeze in patent freezer.

The consistence is quite unlike a water ice, but delicately smooth, and the color is brilliantly crimson.

FROZEN APRICOTS.

ADAPTED BY E. T. J.

Rub a dozen or two ripe apricots through a sieve. Make the fruit very sweet. Add the juice of one lemon and three pints of water. This quantity will be, when frozen, about three quarts.

If fresh apricots cannot be obtained, the large California apricots, in cans, put up by the Golden Gate Packing Company, are a very good substitute. One can, using both fruit and syrup, with three pints of cold water, will make nearly a gallon of ice. Very little additional sugar will be required, and the lemon juice should be used.

FROZEN PEACHES.
ADAPTED BY E. T. J.

This can only be made of fresh peaches, those in cans being unfit for substitute.

Rub the peaches through a sieve—a wire sieve will do, since there are no seeds to remove. Add enough sugar to make very sweet, the juice of one lemon, and three pints of water, and freeze. After the fruit is frozen, but not repacked, eight very ripe, fresh peaches, peeled and cut in small bits, may be stirred in.

Twelve fine peaches, with the above quantity of water, will make over three quarts of ice.

PEACH ICE.
MRS. JOHN BURNHAM.

Take a can of Richardson & Robbins' peaches, which are put up in dry sugar. Rub them through a fine sieve. Make them quite sweet. Add a little lemon juice, to bring out the flavor, and the well-beaten whites of three eggs. Freeze in patent freezer.

FROZEN RASPBERRIES AND BLACKBERRIES.

MRS. JOHN C. WHITE.

Proceed as for frozen strawberries. If desired, a quart of firm, ripe berries, well sugared, but which have not been standing, can be lightly stirred into the ice, after it is frozen, but before repacking.

FROZEN PINEAPPLE.

MRS. JOHN C. WHITE.

Pare carefully a large pineapple, removing all the pits and tough sections. Grate it into a large dish, carefully avoiding the stringy fibre about the core. Make the fruit very sweet, using a pound and a half of sugar at least. Add the juice of one lemon and three pints of cold water. This will make nearly a gallon of fruit ice. When frozen, it will be perfectly white, thick, and soft, like cream ice.

SWEETMEATS AND PICKLES.

SOUTHERN SWEETMEATS.

MRS. HABERSHAM.

SOUTHERN housekeepers have the secret of preserving fruit whereby it retains its shape and color, without the loss which continuous cooking entails. The process is, in fact, merely a return to the methods of our grandmothers, and experience proves that the additional labor is well repaid by the results.

In the case of figs or oranges, two days' immersion in brine is necessary, but the subsequent steps are the same for all fruits preserved whole.

For all fruit, save strawberries, raspberries, blackberries, allow a pound of sugar to a pound of fruit, which must, of course, be very carefully looked over, all which, while not positively injured, are soft, being rejected. Over ripe fruit will never keep, however carefully preserved. Make a syrup of the sugar and a very little water, in the preserving kettle. When near boiling point, put in the fruit; and it is better to do this in instalments, a part at one time, to avoid breaking. Let it boil gently three minutes, remove from syrup with a skimmer, place in a deep dish or jar. Cook the rest in the same way, and, lastly, pour over the whole the hot syrup, and allow it to remain in it two days. In that time the half-cooked fruit will absorb the syrup and become plump, preserving its shape as it can in no other way. On the third day, pour off the syrup into the kettle. When at boiling point, put in as much fruit as will cover the surface of the liquid, let it cook very gently and slowly until quite clear, take out the fruit with a skimmer or fork, fill the jars two-thirds full, and let them stand in a warm place. Cook in this way the balance of the fruit, and when all is removed from the syrup, boil it quickly for five or ten minutes, skimming carefully. Set the jars, one at a time, in a pan of boiling water on the stove, pouring a little hot syrup in each, to prevent the unequal expansion of the glass. Fill up each to overflowing, and screw on the cover, removing it then at once from the water, and screwing it tighter.

SMALL FRUITS.

MRS. HABERSHAM.

The small fruits, of which jams are made, although not requiring such careful treatment, are better to be partially cooked and put away for a day or two. Allow three-quarters of a pound of sugar to one of fruit, put over the fruit and sugar together, let it slowly come to boiling point, boil two or three minutes, then set it away. The third day, boil slowly until the fruit is clear and the whole mass somewhat thick. Under the old process, the fruit was stewed down to the consistency of jam, then put up in small jars or tumblers, with a thin paper laid over it, and a cloth pasted over the top. The long boiling, however, does certainly injure the fruit flavor, and the above method is preferable. Put the sweetmeats into glass jars as directed above.

APPLE SWEETMEATS.

MRS. C. A. TERRY.

Pare, core, and quarter greenings, pippens, or king apples. Weigh them, and allow a half pound of sugar to one pound of apple. Make a syrup of two quarts of water to three pounds of sugar. When boiling, drop in enough apples to cover the surface of the kettle. Let them cook slowly until clear. Put them into the glass jars, filling each half full. Set them where the sweetmeats will keep warm. Drop more apples into the syrup. When six pounds of apple are cooked, set each jar (half full of preserved apples) into a saucepan of boiling water; fill up with the boiling syrup, and screw on the covers, removing immediately from the stove. Make fresh syrup, and proceed with more quartered apple, as before. If fine apples are used, this sweetmeat will be found delicious. It can be used for apple meringue.

BRANDY PEACHES.

CLARK, OF NEW YORK CITY, CONFECTIONER.

Choose ripe but not soft peaches—Morris whites are best. Allow for each jar as many peaches as will fill it one and a half times. Prepare a weak solution of pearl-ash and water; drop the peaches in for a long enough time to allow of the skin being rubbed off. Rub it off carefully with a linen cloth, dropping the peach into a bowl of cold water. It will be better for two persons than one to attend to this process. As quickly as possible remove the peaches; boil them gently in clear water until the flesh of the peach seems loosened from the stone, taking great care not to allow the fruit to be broken nor to become soft.

Drain carefully with a skimmer from the water, and fill the jars with the peaches to the brim. Allow a pound of sugar to each pound of fruit. Scatter the sugar in layers between the peaches in the jar. Fill up the jar with white brandy. Seal carefully.

In making brandy peaches, pure spirit can be used.

PICKLED PINEAPPLE.

MRS. WM. J. BOARDMAN.

To six pounds of thoroughly ripe pineapples allow three pounds of sugar, a quart of vinegar, two ounces of clove, and two ounces of stick cinnamon. Cut the pineapple, after paring it, into small squares; place these in a stone jar; make a syrup of the sugar, vinegar, and spices, and pour it over the pineapple while boiling hot. Repeat this process three successive days, then cover tightly to exclude the air.

GREEN TOMATO PICKLE.

MRS. SHELDON PEASE.

One peck of green tomatoes, sliced thin, stems removed. Let them stand two days in strong brine, changing it daily. Drain off the brine. Add to the tomato twelve onions, peeled and sliced, two ounces of the prepared mixed spices. Nearly cover the pickles in the kettle with vinegar. Let them cook very gently, on the back of the stove, until slightly tender. Put into glass jars (pint), standing the jars, while filling, in boiling water, to repel the air, then screwing on cover and removing at once from fire.

SALADS AND SALAD DRESSINGS.

CHICKEN SALAD.

E. T. J.

RECEIPTS for making chicken salad are to be found in every cook book, and the present rule is only designed to show how expeditiously it can be made, if haste is necessary.

To make chicken salad for twenty-five people, take a two-pound can of Richardson & Robbins' compressed chicken. Although it costs seventy-five cents a pound, as every bit of it can be used, it is really not more expensive than ordinary chicken, while the truffles and jelly in the compressed chicken add to the flavor of the salad. The only thing to be removed is the skin. Cut the chicken down through in slices, and these into dice. Add to it twice as much celery, cut in small bits. Marinate the mixture with three tablespoonfuls of vinegar to nine tablespoonfuls of oil. If this is not enough liquid to pervade the whole mass, add more oil and vinegar in the proportion of one spoonful of vinegar to three of oil. Season it to taste with salt. Just before going to table, pour over it the mayonnaise, which, if made by the receipt given on page 116, for the Keystone egg-beater dressing, renders the whole process a very simple and expeditious one.

The cream dressing for which the receipt is given below, is still better than mayonnaise for chicken salad.

SOUTHERN SALAD.

MRS. GEORGE BELKNAP.

Choose the hearts only of young lettuces; pile them high in your salad bowl; pour over the lettuce a mayonnaise dressing, and scatter over the whole a shower of white or red rose leaves, or place on the top of the pile a handful of English violets, serving some of the flowers with the lettuce.

CREAM DRESSING.

DELMONICO.

Rub together, in a china bowl, a large tablespoonful of butter, four tablespoonfuls of vinegar, a half teaspoonful of salt, and a saltspoonful of flour of mustard. The mustard can be omitted, if objected to. Place the bowl in a saucepan of boiling water, over a spirit lamp or on the stove. Stir the mixture carefully until very hot, to prevent the butter oiling. When sufficiently hot, add two well-beaten eggs, stir until thick, then pour in a cup of cream. Stir until smooth, remove from fire, and allow it to get perfectly cold.

This dressing, which is a modification of a receipt of Delmonico's, is suitable for any salad.

CREAM DRESSING, No. 2.

E. T. J.

The previous receipt can be modified in several ways, and, indeed, can be made very good without cream.

Rub together one tablespoonful of butter, three tablespoonfuls of vinegar, and a teaspoonful of tarragon vinegar, if desired, a half teaspoonful of salt, and a saltspoonful of mustard. Place in a china bowl, in a saucepan of boiling water, and stir until very hot. Add to it two well-beaten eggs, and, when the mixture is thick, remove from the fire, adding a cup of cream, which, if sour, is still better, care being taken that it is merely turned, and not old or cheesy.

If no cream can be had, the quantity of butter can be doubled, and three-quarters of a cup of milk used.

The mixture should be well beaten when the cream is added, then set on ice, stirring occasionally. It will keep for some time in a glass jar.

An excellent salad is made by chopping fine, firm

white cabbage, or the small imported cabbages brought in the spring, and using the cream dressing upon it.

The dressing is especially good for any green salad, even for lettuce, where mayonnaise is not suitable.

Sour milk is preferable to sweet milk in making the dressing.

MAYONNAISE DRESSING.

KEYSTONE EGG-BEATER RECEIPTS.

The introduction of the Keystone egg beater has revolutionized the art of making mayonnaise dressing. The former tedious process has now given place to the work of four or five minutes.

Put into the glass receptacle of the Keystone beater a teaspoonful of salt, a saltspoonful of mustard, the yolks of two raw eggs, and a gill (a sherry glassful) of oil. Turn it a minute, add a gill of oil and a teaspoonful of vinegar, and continue to add these ingredients in the same proportion, beating the mixture a minute between each addition. The two eggs will take about a quart of oil, if necessary. The dressing will take only five minutes to make, and is like yellow jelly.

SAUCES.

TOMATO CATSUP.

ADAPTED BY E. T. J.

Take a gallon of ripe tomatoes, cut them in quarters, removing the stem and green parts. Stew them slowly until quite soft, but not until disintegrated, with six large onions, cut in quarters. Strain through a sieve or tin fruit strainer. To every gallon of liquid add two tablespoonfuls of salt, one and a half tablespoonfuls of ground black pepper, two tablespoonfuls flour of mustard, a tablespoonful ground allspice, a half tablespoonful of cloves, a very little red pepper.

Boil all together, slowly, for an hour, until tolerably thick. Add a pint of vinegar to each gallon of liquid, pour through a funnel into pint ale bottles. Seal with wax, and keep in a cool place. It will require to be shaken before decanting into the cruet, and is better the third than the first year after making.

TOMATO SAUCE.

MRS. VAN REED.

Put into a hot saucepan a tablespoonful of butter, and when it begins to brown, put in it a small onion, chopped fine. Fry a light brown, turn into it a pint of tomatoes, cut fine, or half a can of tomatoes, half a teacup of bread crumbs, a quarter teaspoonful of salt, a little pepper. Let it stew gently, on the back of the stove, an hour. Strain through a medium-sized strainer into a hot saucepan, or over the dish for which it is designed. A little stock added before straining improves it, but, in that case, more bread crumbs must be used.

BROWN SAUCE.

MISS PARLOA.

Heat three tablespoonfuls butter in a frying pan, and when it begins to turn brown, add two tablespoonfuls flour. Stir over the fire until smooth and dark-colored, put on back of stove, and add one and a half cupfuls stock. If you have no stock, use milk or water, or both. Stir until it boils, then simmer three minutes. Season with half a teaspoonful salt, one-eighth teaspoonful pepper, and one tablespoonful tomato catsup. This sauce, especially used for a timbale made of cold meat, can be flavored with chopped mushrooms, which have been previously stewed (whole) gently for an hour in the stock. As the liquid will diminish in bulk, use two full cups of stock. Mushrooms which are canned are unfit for use unless so stewed, being otherwise tough as white kid.

CREAM SAUCE.

MISS C. M. ELY.

Add to drawn butter a teacup of cream, with a little mace and nutmeg to flavor it. Use with boiled fowl.

WHITE SAUCE.

MRS. GEORGE WILLIAMSON SMITH.

Put a large tablespoonful of butter in a hot saucepan; stir it over the fire until bubbling; add two teaspoonfuls of flour. Cook until quite smooth; stir in two-thirds of a pint of hot milk, or milk and water; add salt, and, just before taking from the fire, one well-beaten egg. If to be used for macaroni, add a tablespoonful of grated Parmesan cheese. If for fish or boiled fowl, add chopped hard-boiled eggs, or a dozen oysters, which should be stewed five minutes.

FISH SAUCE.

Make drawn butter as in preceding receipt ; just before serving, add two teaspoonfuls lemon-juice. Water should be used for this sauce instead of milk.

MISCELLANEOUS.

FRITTERS.

MRS. JAMES BIDDLE.

One quart sifted flour. Pour over it, slowly, one quart of boiling water, stirring all the time. Four eggs, beaten light and stirred into the batter, when it becomes cool; a half teaspoonful of salt. Fry in boiling lard. A large quantity of lard is necessary.

CHOCOLATE CARAMELS.

MISS E. W. CLOSSON.

Two cups of sugar; three-fourths cup of butter; half cup grated chocolate (Baker's); one cup warm water. Boil, without stirring, until the syrup will snap in cold water. Pour in a pan, and, when pretty cold, score in squares.

CHOCOLATE.

MISS EVARTS.

The best sweetened chocolate must be used. Break the cakes in pieces, and set in a warm place to melt; put it then into a farina kettle, pouring over it boiling milk and stirring constantly. Serve in cups, and cap with whipped cream.

The proportion of chocolate depends upon the quality desired. To make very thick chocolate, a quarter pound to each half pint of milk is not too much.

KOUMISS OR KUMYS.

MISS C. M. ELY.

To each bottle of fresh cow's milk add two teaspoonfuls of home-made yeast, or one teaspoonful of distillery yeast; sweeten with brown sugar or malt; cork the bottles tightly at once, and set in the refrigerator. The bottles must be of the patent kind used for lager beer. The yeast and sugar may be put in the above proportions into each bottle of milk, which is then corked and wired, instead, as formerly, allowing it to rise before bottling.

It can be used in three days, but is given as a remedy when from four to eight days old.

SAGO JELLY.

DR. WEBSTER, U. S. A.

Mix well together two tablespoonfuls sago, the juice and rind of half a lemon, and one pint of water. Sweeten to taste. Let it stand half an hour, then let it boil, stirring occasionally till clear. Then add two tablespoonfuls of wine, and pour into a mould.

WINE WHEY.

DR. WEBSTER.

Boil a half pint of milk, and, when boiling, add one wineglass of sherry wine. Strain through a sieve, only allowing the whey to run through. Sweeten to taste, and grate upon it a little nutmeg.

BEEF TEA.

DR. WEBSTER.

Chop fine one pound of round steak, carefully removing all fat. Put it into a saucepan, with a pint of cold water. Let it simmer on the hearth or on the back of the stove for two hours. Remove then to a hot place, and boil quickly for half an hour. Season with salt.

CREAM OATMEAL.

ADAPTED BY E. T. J.

Boil oatmeal an hour, as for the table. Strain it then through a sieve, add a little milk to it, and cook it very slowly, in a double boiler, for half an hour more. When perfectly smooth, add a little salt and a little cream.

It is the most delicate food that an invalid can take.

HAIR TONIC.

DR. C. A. TERRY.

One drachm sugar of lead; one drachm lac sulphur; eight ounces bay rum; four ounces Jamaica rum; two ounces glycerine; one teaspoonful salt; one pint warm rainwater. Shake well, and repeat before using.

This is the best preparation for the hair that can be made.

ENGLISH HAIR WASH.

MRS. JUDGE PARKER.

Four ounces bay rum; two ounces whiskey; one ounce glycerine; one-third ounce tincture cantharides; half drachm tannin.

COLD CREAM.

MRS. JAMES BIDDLE.

Two and one-third ounces oil of sweet almonds; one and one-third ounces spermaceti; half ounce of white wax; one ounce rose or orange flower water; a few drops oil of neroli. Melt, and, when it begins to cool, add the perfume, and beat till cold.

FURNITURE POLISH.

MRS. THOS. BELKNAP.

Two pints of sweet oil, one pint of vinegar. Shake well together, in a bottle, and apply with a woolen rag.

www.ingramcontent.com/pod-product-compliance
Lightning Source LLC
Chambersburg PA
CBHW020124170426
43199CB00009B/633